*International Trade and Development*

# International

# Trade and Development

## Gerald M. Meier

CHESTER D. HUBBARD PROFESSOR OF ECONOMICS

WESLEYAN UNIVERSITY

HARPER & ROW, PUBLISHERS, NEW YORK AND EVANSTON

*For Gretl*

The opening of a foreign trade . . . sometimes works a sort of industrial revolution in a country whose resources were previously undeveloped . . .
—John Stuart Mill, *Principles of Political Economy*

The causes which determine the economic progress of nations belong to the study of international trade . . .
—Alfred Marshall, *Principles of Economics*

International trade changes the fundamental facts of economic life in trading nations, and cannot fail to affect in a thousand and one ways the factors governing the output of labor and capital. The far-reaching nature of the indirect influence is best realized if we ask what the world's population and the capital equipment would be like if there had been no international trade, and how different it would be from the present situation.
—Bertil Ohlin, *Interregional and International Trade*

# Contents

# *Preface*

By the very nature of its ambitious sweep, the subject of economic development is only too prone to diffuseness in its increasingly voluminous body of literature. There is a periodic need for studies that bring order to the various branches of the subject. This is especially true now for the international economics of development. Discussions of the connection between trade and development require greater analytical coherency; central issues must be clarified, and major insights consolidated. I have kept these objectives in mind in writing this book.

In so doing, I have found that the traditional theory of international trade, when suitably extended, provides the most useful analytical framework for bringing unity to a variety of observations on the trade problems of poor countries. I have not been convinced by the common criticism that theory in the classical tradition lacks relevance and realism for matters of development. On the contrary, the most pertinent statements about the relations between trade and development retain continuity with traditional trade theory. If its static assumptions are relaxed and additional variables introduced, traditional trade theory can still offer a powerful set of fundamental principles for illuminating development questions.

To this end, I have reconsidered from the standpoint of international development the main topics in the pure theory and monetary theory of international trade. Individual chapters analyze the changing structure of comparative costs in the course of development, the significance for poor countries of secular movements in their terms of trade, the relations between capital formation and the maintenance of balance of payments equilibrium, the developmental role of international capital movements, the use of commercial policy as a component of development programming, and the potential for transmitting development through foreign trade.

I am indebted to the John Simon Guggenheim Memorial Foundation for enabling me to consider portions of this study as a by-product of a larger project that I began while a Guggenheim Fellow. The hospitality of the Oxford University Institute of Statistics and my discussions with members of its staff and other Oxford economists are gratefully remembered. I have also benefited from the opportunity to lecture on an early draft of parts of this book at an Advanced Refresher Course in Economic Development held in Pakistan under the auspices of the International Economic Association and the Pakistan Economic Association.

I should also like to make explicit my special debt to Professors Gottfried Haberler, Harry Johnson, Hla Myint, and the late Ragnar Nurkse. Their writings have done much to enrich the subject-matter of international trade and development, and no amount of footnoting could adequately indicate how strongly influenced I have been by their contributions. I also wish to recall my indebtedness to Professor J. R. Hicks, who first guided my interest in this subject.

Professors Bela Balassa, Gottfried Haberler, and Harry Johnson have been kind enough to read and to criticize most helpfully various parts of the manuscript; I have profited greatly from their suggestions. Needless to say, I alone remain responsible for any errors or negligences.

I am also appreciative for the secretarial services of Miss Catherine E. Cooney and for the financial aid extended by the Research Fund of Wesleyan University.

For permission to use portions of some earlier articles by the author, acknowledgments are due to the editors of the following journals: *Economia Internazionale, Oxford Economic Papers, Panjab University Economist,* and *Social and Economic Studies.*

G. M. M.

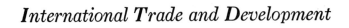

*International Trade and Development*

# 1 Introductory

**1.** The classical theory of international trade has shown a
remarkable capacity to absorb modifications as required by
advances in general economic theory and by the exigencies
of public policy issues. Yet, in spite of its substantial evolution from Hume and Ricardo through Marshall, Edgeworth,
and Taussig, to Viner and Haberler, the traditional theory
still remains an analysis of full static equilibrium with respect
to domestic market assumptions, and is concerned most directly with rich advanced economies. In contrast, general
economic theory has sought increasingly to incorporate long-
period dynamic analysis, and the most pressing international
economic problems now involve the acceleration of development in poor countries.

Followers of the classical tradition have long been uneasy
about Professor Williams' criticism that "the relation of international trade to the development of new resources and productive forces is a more significant part of the explanation of

the present status of nations, of incomes, prices, well-being, than is the cross-section value analysis of the classical economists, with its assumption of given quanta of productive factors, already existent and employed."[1]

More recently, Gunnar Myrdal has observed that "In the complex of tensions between the peoples in the underdeveloped countries, on the one hand, and the industrially advanced ones, on the other, there is an important intellectual element: a suspicion by people in the former countries that in their only recently challenged monopoly of advanced economic analysis, the economists in the latter countries have viewed matters too exclusively from the point of view of their own nations' circumstances and interests, which are not always those of the peoples in the underdeveloped countries."[2] According to Myrdal, "it should not surprise us that, on the whole, the literature is curiously devoid of attempts to relate the facts of international inequalities and the problems of underdevelopment and development to the theory of international trade."[3]

It is true that Myrdal takes an extreme position in his condemnation of the "strange isolation of the theory of international trade from the facts of economic life,"[4] but economists are still generally desirous that trade theory should have more to say about developmental problems. Many would subscribe to Professor Nurkse's more moderate statement: "The case for international specialization is firmly based on considerations of economic efficiency. The world is

[1] J. H. Williams, "The Theory of International Trade Reconsidered," *Economic Journal*, June, 1929, p. 196.

[2] Gunnar Myrdal, *An International Economy*, Harper & Brothers, 1956, p. 222.

[3] Gunnar Myrdal, *Rich Lands and Poor*, Harper & Brothers, 1957, p. 153.

[4] *Ibid.*, p. 154.

not rich enough to be able to despise efficiency. The optimum pattern of specialization is governed by the principle of comparative advantage. This principle remains as valid today as it was in Ricardo's time. And yet there is some question whether it alone can give all the guidance needed by countries whose dominant and deliberate aim is economic development . . . If one asks what help it offers here and now to low-income countries in search of development, the answer is not altogether clear."[5]

These criticisms, together with the widespread interest in development problems at both the theoretical and policy levels, make it apparent that classical theory needs amendment and extension. Although the classicists were attentive to the long-run growth of the domestic economy, they were content to analyze the international economy in essentially static terms. Classical and neoclassical writers did not completely ignore the developmental effects of international trade, but their allusions to developmental topics were quite subsidiary. Their statements on international development have been considered as merely in the nature of *obiter dicta* alongside what has become accepted as the main corpus of traditional trade theory.

For an examination of the poor countries in the international economy, traditional trade theory need not be completely supplanted; but it must be supplemented in a broader frame of reference and removed from the confines of full static equilibrium, as in classical analysis, and from the short period of the cycle, as in Keynesian analysis. It needs to pose a different set of questions. This study presents such an extension.

[5] Ragnar Nurkse, "International Trade Theory and Development Policy," in H. S. Ellis, ed., *Economic Development for Latin America*, St. Martin's Press, 1961, pp. 234, 235.

In adapting traditional theory to deal with phenomena of change, we shall use, in large part, the method of comparative statics. Although we shall refer as much as possible to the underlying dynamics of international development problems, we shall do so in a manner that is short of a truly dynamic analysis of the time-path of the process of change. It is, however, only too easy to make excessive claims for the use of dynamic analysis; dynamic model-building in this area remains a matter of aspiration rather than accomplishment.[6] Our more modest approach should still carry us quite a way in clarifying the international economics of development, even though the desirability of applying a thorough dynamic analysis will be apparent for some of the issues we consider.

**2.**    Our starting point is the simple recognition that at any given time the international economy will be composed of countries which have attained different levels of development as measured by per capita real income. Over a period of time the several countries will also experience differential rates of advance. Moreover, each country's pattern of internal development may vary, in accordance with particular leading and lagging sectors and different interconnections between the sectors.

Once these differences in the level, rate, and pattern of development are recognized, we must transform many of the "constants" in classical trade theory into variables. In the context of development, we can no longer allow resources to be fixed in supply, tastes constant, technical knowledge given, and imports equal to exports with no international capital movements. Such restrictive conditions preclude an analysis of the long-run evolution of international trade and

---

[6] Cf. Richard E. Caves, *Trade and Economic Structure*, Harvard University Press, 1960, pp. 242-244.

ignore the very essence of the development process. If we are to analyze relationships between international trade and development, we must consider the effects of continual increases in productive factors, the evolution of demand conditions, technical progress, and international capital movements. These changes affect international trade, and international trade, in turn, influences the development process. The international economics of development is concerned with these reciprocal relationships.

3.   Such relationships have some relevance for every developing country, whether rich or poor, but they apply with particular force to poor countries. Although there have been studies of the effects of international trade on the maintenance of growth in rich countries, and of the impact of overseas development on the trade of industrial countries, there has been relatively little systematic consideration of the more urgent problem of the effects of trade on the acceleration of development in poor countries. In striving for simplicity, most of the theories of development have sacrificed relevance by abstracting from the international setting in which the national development of poor countries must occur.

The economy of a poor country can be characterized as being an "export economy" or a "dependent economy." These terms may be somewhat arbitrary, and the latter is needlessly emotive, but most of the poor countries do have a strong orientation towards foreign trade. This orientation appears in many ways: a high ratio of export production to total output in the cash sector of the economy, a concentrated structure of export production, a high marginal propensity to import, the inflow of long-term capital, the presence of foreign-owned enterprises, and even in the large share of government revenue derived from customs receipts.

It is also an historical feature of the intersectoral pattern of production that export production has normally displayed the most rapid expansion and that the level of exports has tended to have more influence on aggregate demand than has private investment or government expenditure. The weight of exports in relation to total activity is especially great for the poor or the smaller nations.[7] And even though the ratio of foreign trade to national income is usually low in a predominantly subsistence economy before the pace of development accelerates, the ratio rises rapidly with development as foreign trade tends to grow faster than income in the early stages of development.[8] On both quantitative and qualitative grounds, it is therefore especially important to examine the development of poor countries in the context of their external environment.

**4.**  In doing this, we may focus on four basic problems:

**a.**  If we determine how the structure of comparative advantage changes over time, we can then ask how the volume and composition of trade and the gains from trade undergo change. Traditional trade theory does not provide an immediate answer to this, insofar as it is restricted to the narrower questions of what commodities would be traded and what would be the gains from trade at a given moment. To extend this analysis to a developing economy we must consider how

[7] On the basis of data presented by Professor Kuznets, it is clear that the smaller the country, as measured by population, the larger is the ratio of exports or imports to total output, and that foreign trade is more important relative to total output for smaller rather than larger countries. Simon Kuznets, "Economic Growth of Small Nations," in E. A. G. Robinson, ed., *The Economic Consequences of the Size of Nations*, St. Martin's Press, 1960, pp. 18-20.

[8] W. A. Lewis, *The Theory of Economic Growth*, George Allen & Unwin Ltd., 1955, p. 342.

changes in factor supplies, technical progress, increasing productivity, and changes in demand can transform the structure of comparative costs. We examine these developmental aspects of the pure theory of trade in Chapter 2, which introduces long period changes into the theory of comparative costs, and in Chapter 3, which investigates the long period determinants of the terms of trade.

**b.** In considering the monetary theory of trade, we should relate the problem of maintaining balance of payments equilibrium to the developmental problem of capital accumulation. Chapter 4 does this by analyzing the possible sources of conflict between the objectives of accelerating capital formation and preserving external balance.

**c.** It is also essential to relate international investment to the development process. The traditional theory of international capital movements focuses on the transfer problem and the mechanism of adjustment in the balance of payments. But the transfer of productive capital and its interconnection with the forces of development receive only slight attention. Chapter 5 attempts to remedy this deficiency by examining some developmental aspects of the international movement of capital.

**d.** Finally, we should seek an answer to the overriding question of whether there is a conflict between the gains from trade and the gains from growth—whether the process of development is facilitated or handicapped through international trade. To what extent can the foreign sector transmit developmental forces to a poor country? Is free trade the optimal trade policy for stimulating development, or can development be more readily accelerated by the use of restrictive commercial policy? Should poor countries concentrate on export stimulation or import replacement? In what ways can the process of growth-transmission through foreign trade be accelerated? Chapters 6 and 7 discuss such questions.

**5.** Each of these problems has attracted increasing attention in the recent literature of international trade and economic development. The contributions remain, however, dispersed and rather fragmentary. The time has come to consolidate these various contributions and extend them within the main corpus of international trade theory.

# 2  *Comparative Costs*

1.  The pure theory of international trade has been most thoroughly refined in terms of static general equilibrium analysis. This analysis, with its emphasis on the relations between production and trade and its formulation of the doctrine of comparative costs, is a convenient starting point for our subsequent discussion.

To recall the leading principles of this analysis we may concentrate on the usual two-country, two-commodity, two-factor model.[1] This is the simplest possible model which contains the fundamental elements of the general equilibrium problem, but the inferences drawn from it will, for the most

[1] Cf. Gottfried Haberler, "Some Problems in the Pure Theory of International Trade," *Economic Journal,* June, 1950, pp. 223-240; James E. Meade, *A Geometry of International Trade,* George Allen & Unwin Ltd., 1952, chaps. I-V; Kelvin Lancaster, "The Heckscher-Ohlin Trade Model: A Geometric Treatment," *Economica,* February, 1957, pp. 19-39; Richard E. Caves, *Trade and Economic Structure,* Harvard University Press, 1960, chap. II.

part, be essentially the same as those of a multicountry, multi-commodity, multifactor model.

Let the countries be $E$ and $G$, the commodities $X$ and $Y$, and the factors labor $(L)$ and capital $(C)$. We assume that (1) purely competitive conditions prevail in product and factor markets; (2) the production functions of $X$ and $Y$ are subject to constant returns to scale; (3) $X$ is always the more "labor-intensive" industry, in the sense that, at the same relative prices for the factors in both industries, the ratio of total labor to total capital used in the production of $X$ is greater than the corresponding ratio in the production of $Y$; and (4) in each country the factor supplies are fixed in total amount, and technical knowledge, labor efficiency, consumer tastes, and the distribution of income between factors are all held constant. After summarizing the static analysis, we shall remove assumption (4) and introduce various long period changes into our discussion.

2.   Consider country $E$. In an Edgeworth-Bowley box diagram of production functions for country $E$, as in Fig. 1, the locus of the points of the two sets of isoquants forms an "efficiency locus" $XY$ which represents optimal resource allocation for the production of $X$ and $Y$ with given supplies of $L$ and $C$ in country $E$. This follows from the fact that at each point of tangency the ratio between the marginal productivities of $L$ and $C$ (given by the slope of the isoquants) in the production of $X$ is equal to the ratio between their marginal productivities in the production of $Y$. Production is then efficient in the sense that it is impossible to produce more of one commodity without reducing the output of the other.

By reading off the amounts of $X$ and $Y$ along the efficiency locus and translating these amounts to a plane such as in Fig. 2, we derive the "production frontier" (transformation curve

or production-possibility curve) *MN*. This curve represents
the maximum-possible combinations of *X* and *Y* that can be
produced in country *E*. Its position follows from the conditions of factor supply and production functions indicated in
Fig. 1. The slope of *MN* at any point denotes the ratio of the
marginal opportunity costs of *X* and *Y*, the marginal opportunity cost of producing an additional unit of one commodity

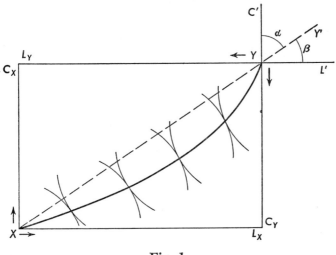

Fig. 1.

being measured by the necessary reduction in the output of
the other. In Fig. 2, the production frontier is concave to the
origin, indicating that the marginal opportunity cost of transforming one commodity into the other is increasing as more
of the commodity is produced.[2]

[2] Cf. W. F. Stolper and P. A. Samuelson, "Protection and Real
Wages," *Review of Economic Studies*, November, 1941, pp. 58-73;
Caves, *op. cit.*, pp. 30-35. The production frontier is concave in Fig. 2,
even though it is assumed that constant returns to scale exist in the

**3.**  If we are now given the conditions of domestic demand, represented for simplicity by community indifference curves $I_1 \cdots I_4$ in Fig. 2, we can determine the equilibrium posi-

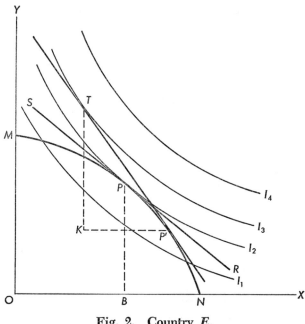

Fig. 2.  Country $E$.

production of each commodity, because different factor proportions are used in the production of $X$ and $Y$; if the production of one good expands, it must then use factors in a more costly combination. With constant returns in the production functions, the production frontier is concave to a degree depending on the elasticities of substitution.

If constant returns exist in the production of each good, and each production process uses factors in exactly the same ratio at any given factor-price ratio, the production frontier would be a straight line, indicating that the marginal opportunity cost of transforming one good into the other remained constant. If, however, the production functions were sufficiently strongly subject to increasing returns, the frontier would be convex to the origin, indicating that the marginal cost of $X$ in terms of $Y$ falls as more of $X$ is produced.

tion of country $E$ before trade.[3] The domestic exchange ratio
or its reciprocal, the price ratio, is given by the slope of $RS$
in Fig. 2. Market equilibrium for the closed economy is then
at $P$, the point of tangency between the production frontier
and a community indifference curve. At $P$ the following equilibrium conditions hold: in the factor markets, the ratio of
the marginal product of labor to the marginal product of
capital is the same in each occupation, and the price of each
factor is equal to its marginal value product. In the commodity markets, the price ratio is equal to the marginal cost
ratio (the slope of $RS$ equals the slope of the production
frontier at $P$). The price ratio is also equal to the marginal
rate of substitution in consumption (as given by the slope of
the community indifference curve at $P$), and the consumption of each commodity is equal to its output ($OB$ of $X$ and
$BP$ of $Y$). Moreover, the position of market equilibrium is an
optimum: it is on the production frontier, and the relative
valuation of the products by consumers is equal to the relative costs of production to society (the marginal rate of
substitution in consumption equals the marginal rate of
transformation in production).

A similar analysis applies to country $G$. It may be assumed
that the relative endowment of factors differs from that in $E$,
and that $G$'s domestic price ratio is different from $E$'s in the
absence of trade.

4.   Let us now open the countries to trade, and allow an
international price ratio—the terms of trade—to be established
on the world market. When the terms of trade lie between

[3] Community indifference curves are used merely as an heuristic
device, not as an empirical construct or as a basis for conclusions about
changes in economic welfare. Cf. T. Scitovsky, "A Reconsideration of
the Theory of Tariffs," *Review of Economic Studies*, Summer, 1942,
pp. 93-95; P. A. Samuelson, "Social Indifference Curves," *Quarterly
Journal of Economics*, February, 1956, pp. 1-22.

the different domestic price ratios that exist in $E$ and $G$ in the absence of trade, both countries can gain through international specialization and trade. Each country will tend to specialize in the production of the commodity which it can produce relatively cheaply—namely, the commodity which is intensive in its relatively abundant factor—and will demand imports from the other country by supplying exports of this commodity in which it has a comparative advantage.[4] As the terms of trade vary, each country's willingness to trade will change according to its particular production possibilities and preference pattern. The country's willingness to trade can be represented by a Marshallian reciprocal demand curve, or an international trade offer curve. Once we derive each country's offer curve, we can determine the equilibrium terms of trade and the equilibrium volume of exports and imports for each country.

To derive the offer curve for country $E$, we interpret the

[4] Even if factor endowments were identical in both countries, demand conditions could be dissimilar and could cause the domestic price ratios to differ in the absence of trade, so that international trade would still be profitable. See Bertil Ohlin, *Interregional and International Trade*, Harvard University Press, 1933, p. 16; W. W. Leontief, "The Use of Indifference Curves in the Analysis of Foreign Trade," *Quarterly Journal of Economics*, May, 1933, pp. 499-506.

If factor abundance is interpreted narrowly as meaning only "physical" abundance rather than "economic" abundance, it is possible that the influence of demand conditions may also give rise to an exceptional result: differences in tastes may be so great that a country may not export the product which uses relatively more of its abundant factor. The possibility of such a special case is, however, remote, insofar as it is highly unlikely that differences in tastes are so much greater than differences in factor endowment ratios. Cf. Stefan Valavanis-Vail, "Leontief's Scarce Factor Paradox," *Journal of Political Economy*, December, 1954, pp. 525-526; Kelvin Lancaster, "Protection and Real Wages: A Restatement," *Economic Journal*, June, 1957, pp. 208-210; R. W. Jones, "Factor Proportions and the Heckscher-Ohlin Model," *Review of Economic Studies*, vol. 24 (1956-57), pp. 1-5.

terms of trade as a parameter and consider the reactions of $E$ to variations in the terms of trade. If the terms of trade are identical with the domestic exchange ratio in $E$, namely the slope of $RS$ (Fig. 2), $E$ will continue to produce and consume the combination of $X$ and $Y$ indicated at $P$. If, however, the terms of trade diverge from the initial domestic price ratio, production and consumption will be altered, and the domestic production and consumption of each commodity will no longer be equal. The direction and degree of alteration will depend on the extent of the divergence of the international price ratio from the internal price ratio, the shape of the production frontier, and the preference pattern.

If the terms of trade line becomes steeper than the internal price line $RS$, a unit of $X$ will exchange for more units of $Y$ on the world market than on the home market; the country will accordingly specialize in the production of $X$ in which it has a comparative advantage.[5] In contrast, if the terms of trade line becomes less steep than $RS$, a unit of $Y$ will exchange for more units of $X$ on the world market than on the home market, and the country will tend to specialize in the production of $Y$. Thus, in Fig. 2, when the terms of trade line is $P'T$, $E$ specializes in the production of $X$, shifts production to the quantities represented by $P'$, offers for export $P'K$ of $X$ (the excess of domestic production over domestic consumption of $X$) in payment for imports of $KT$ of $Y$ (the excess of domestic consumption over domestic production of $Y$),[6] and

---

[5] "Specialization" involves the production of more of the good whose world price has risen relatively, and less of the good whose price has been lowered relatively on the world market. In the present case, specialization in production is incomplete: the country concentrates relatively in $X$, but still produces both $X$ and $Y$.

[6] We ignore transport costs. The price differences between countries before trade must, of course, be wider than transport costs in order to have trade be profitable.

consumes the quantities represented by $T$. Conforming to the equilibrium conditions of pure competition, the production point $P'$ and the consumption point $T$ are determined by the requirement that the price ratio, marginal cost ratio, marginal rate of transformation in production, and marginal rate of substitution in consumption should all be equal.

We may now derive country $E$'s offer curve, $EE'$ in Fig. 3, by plotting in the first quadrant country $E$'s offers of $X$ for $Y$ at the various terms of trade lines steeper than $RS$, such as $P'T$ in Fig. 2, and by plotting in the third quadrant $E$'s offers of $Y$ for $X$ at the various terms of trade lines less steep than $RS$.[7]

By similar reasoning, we may derive country $G$'s offer curve, $GG'$, in Fig. 3. Only the first quadrant in which the offer curves intersect is of practical interest. If there is free trade, no transport costs and no surplus or deficit in the balance of trade, then the position of trade equilibrium will be at $C$, the point of intersection of the offer curves. This is a position of stable equilibrium.[8] The equilibrium terms of

[7] In Fig. 3, $+ X_E$ and $-X_G$ denote exports of $X$ from $E$ and imports of $X$ into $G$, respectively. Similarly, $+ Y_E$ and $-Y_G$ represent exports of $Y$ from $E$ and imports of $Y$ into $G$, respectively.

[8] Cf. Alfred Marshall, *Money, Credit, and Commerce,* Macmillan & Co., 1923, p. 341. A displacement of the terms of trade from equilibrium would set in motion forces inducing a return to that equilibrium. A change, for instance, in the terms of trade to the right of $OC$ would create an excess demand for $E$'s exports at the lower price, and the relative price of $E$'s exports must then rise. A change to the left of $OC$ would create an excess supply of $E$'s exports at the higher price, and the relative price of $E$'s exports must then fall.

The offer curves we have derived in Fig. 3 resemble, but are not identical with, the Marshallian reciprocal demand curves. Marshall assumed each country "to make up her exports into representative 'bales'; that is, bales each of which represents uniform aggregate investments of her labour and her capital." The Marshallian terms of trade are then factoral instead of commodity terms of trade. Condi-

trade are equivalent to the slope of $OC$; the equilibrium volume of trade is $OM$ of $X$ or $MC$ of $Y$; and $E$'s exports are

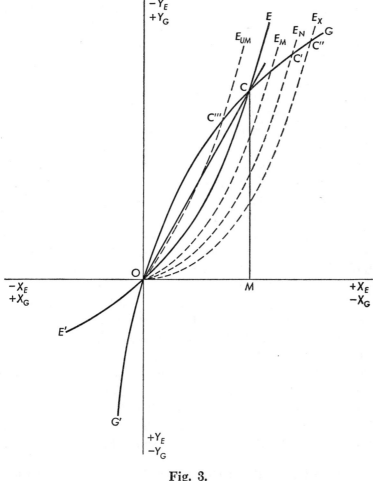

Fig. 3.

tions under which the commodity terms of trade will be equivalent to the double-factoral terms are discussed in Chapter 3, section 2.

equal to $G$'s imports. If in Fig. 2 the trading point $T$ is an
equilibrium trading position for country $E$, the point $T$ must
then lie on $G$'s offer curve at $C$ in Fig. 3, and $OM$ (Fig. 3)
equals $P'K$ (Fig. 2), and $MC$ (Fig. 3) equals $KT$ (Fig. 2).
In the remainder of the discussion, we shall let the equilibrium terms of trade line be $P'T$ (Fig. 2), so that $E$ finds it
profitable to export the labor-intensive commodity $X$.

**5.**    The contribution of international trade to economic welfare can now be readily recognized.[9] The equilibrium trading
conditions, summarized in the previous section, fulfill the optimum conditions of resource allocation. Without any increase in resources, or technological change, each country is
able to enjoy a higher real income by specializing in production according to its comparative advantage and trading. Unless the terms of trade are exactly the same as the rate at
which $X$ can be exchanged for $Y$ at home, the country's access to a foreign market has a real income effect that is essentially the same as if there had been an outward shift in its
production frontier.

If, in Fig. 2, country $E$'s trading position were at some
point on $P'T$ to the right and above the no-trade position $P$,
a larger quantity of both $X$ and $Y$ would actually be gained.
The country's trading position would then be clearly superior
to its no-trade position. If, however, country $E$'s equilibrium
trading position is at $T$ (above but to the left of $P$), then
more $Y$ but less $X$ is available than at $P$. In this case, the col-
lection of goods at $T$ can be shown to be superior to that at
the no-trade situation by a comparison of the quantity index

[9] Excellent summaries of literature on the welfare effects of inter-
national trade are provided by Caves, *op. cit.*, chap. VIII, and E. J.
Mishan, "A Survey of Welfare Economics, 1939-1959," *Economic
Journal,* June, 1960, pp. 197-265.

numbers of the two situations. There is then still a potential increase in welfare, even if trade makes some individuals worse off, while making others better off; a redistribution of the larger product could leave each individual as well or better off than he was before trade.

The increase in the level of satisfaction from trade will depend on the width of the gaps in the comparative advantages of the trading nations and on the differences in their relative demands. The gains from trade will therefore be greater when the less similar are demand conditions, factor proportions, and the technical coefficients of production for different commodities in the different countries. In other words, the greater the differences in the domestic price ratios and in the relative demands of the countries, the wider will be the range in which the international price ratio can diverge from the domestic ratio; the potential increase in satisfaction from the opening of trade will therefore be greater.[10]

**6.**   The foregoing analysis refines the orthodox statement of the comparative cost doctrine in terms of modern general equilibrium theory. It also establishes explicitly the basis for offer curve analysis; the hitherto "unseen movements of the machinery" behind the offer curves, which were of such concern to Marshall and Edgeworth,[11] are now revealed to consist of production, income, and substitution effects as a new production point is taken up on the production frontier in

----

[10] Given its production frontier and preferences, a country will gain more satisfaction from trade, the larger is the price change from the no-trade position. But it should be noted that the gain from trade can not be measured simply by the price movement. See Chapter 3 for a discussion of why, in some cases, an improvement in a country's terms of trade may not be indicative of an improved welfare position.

[11] F. Y. Edgeworth, *Papers Relating to Political Economy*, vol. II, Macmillan & Co., 1925, p. 32.

response to a variation in the terms of trade. Finally, the analysis relates the gains from trade to modern welfare economics by emphasizing an efficient pattern of world production and the equality between relative prices and marginal rates of transformation in production and marginal rates of substitution in consumption.[12]

We can now extend the analysis to development problems by first interpreting a country's development in terms of outward shifts in its production frontier. These shifts can be traced to autonomous changes in factor supply, techniques of production, and labor efficiency. Each particular change will have not only a "production effect" (discussed in sections 7 through 9), but also a "consumption effect" (section 10); together these effects will cause shifts in a country's offer curve. The overall strength of the combined production and consumption effects will determine the direction and extent of the shift in each country's offer curve, and thereby the changes in the volume and composition of trade that will result from particular types of factor accumulation, technological progress, and increased labor efficiency (section 11).[13]

[12] Much of this analysis could also be readily incorporated into the framework of linear programming; the international trade problem of determining optimal outputs by permitting price ratios to change can be interpreted as a particular case of "parametric programming." Cf. Robert Dorfman, P. A. Samuelson, R. M. Solow, *Linear Programming and Economic Analysis,* McGraw-Hill, 1958, pp. 31-38, 41-45, 59-63, 117-121, 346-348; Helen Makower, *Activity Analysis,* Macmillan & Co., 1957, chap. IX; T. M. Whitin, "Classical Theory, Graham's Theory, and Linear Programming in International Trade," *Quarterly Journal of Economics,* November, 1953, pp. 520-544; L. W. McKenzie, "On Equilibrium in Graham's Model of World Trade and Other Competitive Systems," *Econometrica,* April, 1954, pp. 142-161.

[13] An earlier version of this analysis was given in the author's "Note on the Theory of Comparative Costs and Long Period Developments," *Economia Internazionale,* August, 1952, pp. 3-12. In its more extensive

7.  We may first delimit the different types of production effects that will result from various types of factor growth. Introducing changes in the factor supplies of country $E$ will mean that the dimensions of the box diagram in Fig. 1 are no longer fixed, but expand or contract according to whether the factors increase or decrease in supply. Only movements of the box into the quadrant northeast of $Y$ (Fig. 1) are relevant to development problems, for only in this quadrant is the quantity of some or all factors increased without a diminution in others. Movement into any other quadrant involves a decumulation of capital or an absolute reduction in the labor force—not impossible, but certainly exceptional occurrences for a developing economy.

Accordingly, we may identify the following five types of factor accumulation and their respective production effects in country $E$:[14]

a.  A movement along $YY'$ (Fig. 1)—that is, the absolute amounts of the factors increase proportionately over a period so that the relative factor endowment remains the same at the end of the period as it was at the beginning. In terms of Fig. 2, the production frontier would then retain the same shape but would shift out proportionately for both commodities, since the original box diagram would simply be rescaled according to the proportionate increase in factor supplies.

---

form, the present analysis owes much to J. R. Hicks, "An Inaugural Lecture," *Oxford Economic Papers*, June, 1953, pp. 117-125; H. G. Johnson, *International Trade and Economic Growth*, George Allen & Unwin Ltd., 1958, chap. III; Johnson, "Economic Development and International Trade," *Pakistan Economic Journal*, December, 1959, pp. 47-71.

[14] Although the analysis refers to country $E$, which exports the labor-intensive commodity, it is a simple matter of translation to recognize the opposite effects in $G$, which exports the capital-intensive commodity.

The effect on production, at constant prices, will then be the same proportionate increase in the outputs of exportable and importable goods. This can be classified as a "neutral" production effect.[15]

**b.**   A movement into region β (Fig. 1)—that is, labor increases proportionately more than does capital. The family of $Y$-isoquants that originated previously at $Y$ must now be shifted northeastwards to the new origin in region β. This will bring into tangency isoquants that originally neither touched nor intersected, thereby forming a new efficiency locus. The production frontier derived from the new efficiency locus will then lie beyond the initial frontier at all points, and the outward shift of the frontier will be proportionately greater in the direction of the labor-intensive commodity $X$. A proportionately greater increase in the factor which is embodied most intensively in the exportable good $X$ will thus result in the supply of exportables increasing in greater proportion than the supply of importables $Y$. This type of output expansion can be classified as "export-biased."

**c.**   A movement into region α (Fig. 1)—that is, capital in-

---

[15] The terminology "neutral," "export-biased," and "import-biased," is suggested by Hicks, *op. cit.*, pp. 127 ff.; also, Hicks, *Essays in World Economics*, Oxford University Press, 1959, note B. Professor Johnson uses the terminology of "pro-trade-biased" instead of "export-biased," and "anti-trade-biased" instead of "import-biased"; Johnson, *International Trade and Economic Growth, op. cit.*, pp. 76-77. See also, J. Black and P. P. Streeten, "La balance Commerciale les termes de l'échange et la croissance économique," *Économie Appliquée*, April-September, 1957, pp. 299-322.

The difference in terminology is explained by Professor Hicks' concern with whether technical progress occurs in the exporting or import-competing industry, while Professor Johnson is interested in other kinds of changes as well, and the effects of different changes on the demand for imports (supply of exports).

creases proportionately more than does labor. The origin of the isoquant map of $Y$ will be shifted into region $\alpha$, and a new efficiency locus will be formed. The new production frontier derived from this new efficiency locus will then lie beyond the initial frontier at all points, but the outward shift of the frontier will be proportionately greater in the direction of the capital-intensive commodity $Y$. A proportionately greater increase in the factor which is embodied most intensively in the import-competing good $(Y)$ will thus result in the domestic supply of importables increasing in greater proportion than the supply of exportables. This type of output expansion can be classified as "import-biased."

d. A movement along $YL'$ (Fig. 1)—that is, there is an increase in the labor supply without any increase in the quantity of capital. The production effect of this increased labor supply will be to expand the supply of exportables $(X)$ and reduce the domestic supply of importable goods $(Y)$ at constant prices. This type of output expansion can be classified as "ultra-export-biased."

The proof of this production effect depends on the theorem, originally stated by T. M. Rybczynski,[16] that at constant relative prices of the two commodities, an increase in the supply of one factor, with the other factor constant, will result in an absolute expansion in production of the commodity using relatively much of the increased factor, but an absolute reduction in the production of the commodity using relatively little of this factor. In order to absorb the augmented factor at an unchanged price it is necessary to secure

[16] T. M. Rybczynski, "Factor Endowment and Relative Commodity Prices," *Economica*, November, 1955, pp. 336-341. For a mathematical proof of this proposition, see W. M. Corden, "Economic Expansion and International Trade: A Geometric Approach," *Oxford Economic Papers*, June, 1956, p. 227.

more of the other factor as well; this can be achieved only by freeing the other factor from the industry in which it is used intensively, resulting in a contraction of that industry. Stated more precisely, this result follows from the condition that if the ratio of product prices is to be kept constant, then it is also necessary that the ratio of factor prices should remain constant. This, in turn, requires maintenance of the labor:capital ratio that existed initially in each industry; an unchanged factor ratio will keep the relative marginal productivities of the factors constant, and relative factor prices will then remain constant. To maintain, however, a constant factor ratio in the industry which uses the extra factor intensively, it is necessary to free the other factor by contracting the industry which uses it intensively.

Since country $E$ has an initial comparative advantage in the labor-intensive commodity $X$, an increase in labor supply without any capital accumulation will extend production in the direction of $X$. This will be accompanied by a transfer of both labor and capital from the capital-intensive industry $Y$ to industry $X$. But capital will be released from the $Y$-industry in a greater quantity than is required to operate the released labor in the $X$-industry, and this surplus capital will then be available to work with the additional labor. The point on the new efficiency locus with the same labor:capital ratio in $X$ and $Y$, and thereby the same exchange ratio between the factors as existed initially, will involve a larger output of $X$ but a smaller output of $Y$. It follows that the new point of production on the new production frontier, corresponding to the initial price ratio of goods, will entail an absolute increase in the output of the exportable commodity $X$ and an absolute reduction in the output of the importable commodity $Y$. Thus, an increase in labor without any increase in capital will have for country $E$ a production effect that is ultra-export-biased.

e. A movement along $YC'$ (Fig. 1)—that is, the quantity of capital increases without any increase in labor supply. By reasoning similar to that advanced above, the production effect of this capital accumulation will be an increase in the supply of the capital-intensive importable $Y$ and a reduction in the supply of the labor-intensive exportable $X$. Such an output expansion which reduces the domestic production of exportables can be classified as ultra-import-biased.

The five types of production effects due to the different types of factor accumulation in country $E$ can be summarized in simple geometric terms as in Fig. 4.[17] Let the terms of trade line $M''N''$ be drawn parallel to and to the right of $M'N'$, indicating constant relative prices but expanded production. If the path of output expansion from $P'$ is along the straight line $P'L$, the production effect is neutral; the supply of exportables $(X)$ and the supply of importables $(Y)$ increase in the same proportion. If the output expansion line rises to the right of $P'L$, such as $P'X$, the production effect is export-biased; the supply of exportables increases in greater proportion than the supply of importables. If the line rises to the left of $P'L$, such as $P'A$, the production effect is import-biased; the supply of importables increases in greater proportion than the supply of exportables. If it slopes negatively, such as $P'U$, the effect is ultra-export-biased; the domestic production of importables is reduced. And if it slopes negatively in the other direction, such as $P'U'$, the production effect is ultra-import-biased; the supply of exportables is reduced.[18]

[17] Cf. Corden, *op. cit.*, pp. 223, 225.

[18] In formal terms, the production effect may also be defined as "export-biased," "neutral," or "import-biased," according as the "output-elasticity of supply of importable goods" is less than, equal to, or greater than unity; Johnson, *International Trade and Economic Growth, op. cit.*, p. 77. The output-elasticity of supply of importables is defined as the proportional change in quantity of importables

8. Technological progress will also alter the structure of comparative costs. Allowing for this, our analysis must now incorporate the various production effects from different

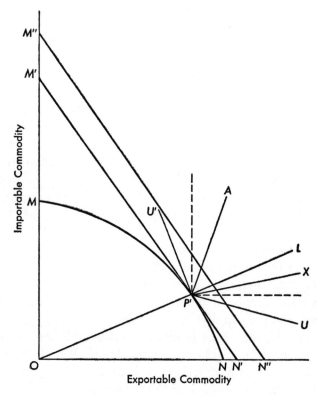

Fig. 4.  Country *E*.

supplied, divided by the proportional change in national output. A negative output-elasticity of supply of importables would denote a production effect that is ultra-export-biased, and a negative output elasticity of supply of exportables would indicate an ultra-import-bias.

types of innovations.[19] A technical innovation may be "labor-saving," in the sense that it lowers the optimal ratio of labor to capital; at the initial factor prices, the cost of producing a given output is then reduced, and the supply of the "saved" factor labor is in effect increased. Or the innovation may be "capital-saving," in the sense that the optimal ratio of capital to labor is lowered at the original relative factor prices; the cost of production is again lowered, and a quantity of the "saved" factor capital is set free. Finally, the innovation may be "neutral," inasmuch as it is neither labor-saving nor capital-saving, but allows a reduction by the same proportion in the amounts of the two factors required to produce a given quantity of output; the optimal factor ratio is unaltered, but the output obtainable from a given combination of factors is increased.

Considering these different types of innovations, we may now ask what type of bias in production will result, according to whether the innovation occurs in industry $X$ or $Y$. In the following cases, we shall concentrate on country $E$ and determine what will be the shift, at constant relative product prices, in the output of one of the commodities as a result of an innovation in the production of the other commodity.

a. A neutral innovation: If this occurs in the labor-intensive industry $X$, the output of $X$ would increase, and at the original relative factor prices its production costs would fall. To have the original product price ratio remain unchanged after this innovation, there must then be a shift in the factor

[19] This problem has been clarified considerably by R. Findlay and H. Grubert, "Factor Intensity, Technological Progress, and the Terms of Trade," *Oxford Economic Papers*, February, 1959, pp. 111-121. A good summary of the effects of biased technical progress is presented in J. Bhagwati and H. G. Johnson, "Notes on Some Controversies in the Theory of International Trade," *Economic Journal*, March, 1960, p. 82.

price ratio. In this case, there would be an incentive for factors to move from industry $Y$ to $X$, where the marginal productivities and factor earnings are higher. When this occurs, the price of labor rises, and the price of capital falls, since capital is used less intensively in $X$ where the innovation has occurred. The relative costs of $X$ and $Y$ are thereby altered, and the initial product price ratio is restored. Thus, at constant relative product prices, the effect of neutral technical progress in the exportable commodity $X$ is to expand the output of $X$ and to contract the output of the importable commodity $Y$.[20] The production effect of a neutral innovation in the export industry is ultra-export-biased.

If, in contrast, the neutral innovation occurred in the production of the importable commodity $Y$, the production effect would be ultra-import-biased.

**b.**   A labor-saving innovation: If this occurs in industry $X$, production costs in $X$ will again be reduced, and a quantity of labor will be released. As in the preceding situation, the reduction in cost requires a shift of resources from $Y$ to the innovating industry $X$. And, as in the case of an increase in the labor supply, the labor set free by the innovation in $X$ must be absorbed by an expansion in the output of the exportable commodity $X$, which uses labor relatively intensively, and by a contraction in the production of importables $Y$. The production effect is therefore ultra-export-biased. Moreover, since in the present case technical progress saves the factor which is used relatively intensively in the production of the exportable commodity $X$, the production effect will be even more ultra-export-biased than if the innovation were neutral.

[20] A rigorous proof of this proposition has been given by J. Bhagwati, "Growth, Terms of Trade, and Comparative Advantage," *Economia Internazionale*, August, 1959, pp. 412-414.

If, however, the labor-saving innovation occurs in the capital-intensive industry $Y$, the production effect may be anywhere between the extremes of ultra-import-biased and ultra-export-biased. This range is possible because the innovation will not only reduce the unit cost of production in $Y$, thereby tending to increase the supply of importables $Y$, but will also release labor from $Y$, thereby tending to increase the supply of exportables $X$, since at constant factor prices the labor that is released from $Y$ must be absorbed by an expansion of the labor-intensive industry $X$. Depending on the respective strengths of the cost-reducing and factor-saving effects which operate in opposite directions, the production effect on balance may vary from being ultra-import-biased to being ultra-export-biased. If the innovation is only slightly labor-saving, the production effect will be ultra-import-biased. But if the innovation is so strongly saving of labor as to offset the substitution effect of cheaper labor, the production effect will be ultra-export-biased.

c.   A capital-saving innovation: If the innovation is in the capital-intensive industry $Y$, then, by reasoning similar to that in the previous case of a labor-saving innovation in $X$, the supply of importables $Y$ will increase at the expense of exportables $X$. The production effect will be ultra-import-biased.

If, however, the capital-saving innovation is in the labor-intensive industry $X$, the production effect may vary from being ultra-export-biased to being ultra-import-biased, depending on how much capital is released by the innovation. Again, in this case, the cost-reducing effect of the innovation and the factor-saving effect work in opposite directions; depending on the balance of these effects, the resultant production effect may vary from being ultra-export-biased to being ultra-import-biased.

**9.**   The production effects from an increase in labor efficiency can be readily incorporated into the analysis already presented for cases of an increase in labor supply or technical progress. Aside from considerations of differences in income distribution and different income effects on demand, an increase in labor efficiency is analytically equivalent to an increase in the supply of labor; it results in the same combination of inputs yielding a greater output than was formerly obtainable, or, alternatively, in allowing the same output to be produced with a smaller amount of labor. This is equivalent to a shift in the production function, each isoquant now representing a larger product. When this is due simply to the greater personal efficiency of labor (for instance, through an improvement of skill) with no dependence whatsoever on technical change and capital accumulation, the greater efficiency would have a production effect identical with that of an increase in labor supply, as analyzed in section 7 (d), above. When, as may be more common, an increase in output per man-hour is due to neutral or labor-saving innovations, the preceding analysis of technical progress is again applicable.

**10.**   We now know how different kinds of factor accumulation, technical progress, and increased labor efficiency will have various production effects. But we must also recognize the effects of these developmental changes on the pattern of consumption. To complete our analysis of the developing country's demand for imports, we must examine the various possible consumption effects and then note the combined effects of the changes in production and consumption.

Considering country $E$, we may first separate out the consumption effect of only an increase in real income if we assume that the preference system remains unchanged, and then recognize how, at constant relative commodity prices,

a new consumption point will be reached as income increases.[21] In Fig. 5, let the initial terms of trade line *M'N'*
be tangential to a community indifference curve at *T*, the

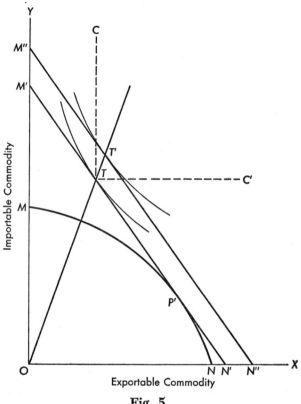

Fig. 5.

initial consumption point. If development now occurs, the
consumption point will shift. Let the terms of trade line

[21] We exclude the possibility that although national income may
increase because of population growth, this may at the same time result in a lower income per head.

$M''N''$ then be drawn parallel to and to the right of $M'N'$, denoting unchanged relative prices but an increase in income after development occurs. If the income-elasticity of demand for $Y$ equals unity, and that for $X$ also equals unity, the new consumption point is $T'$ on the straight line income-consumption curve $OTT'$ drawn through the origin; the ratio of $Y{:}X$ that would be purchased at initial prices is the same after an increase in income as originally. In this case, the expansion of income raises the demand for importables $Y$ in the same proportion as it increases the demand for exportables $X$. The consumption effect can thus be termed "neutral."

Although a neutral income effect is possible, this will not generally be the case. Instead, the income-consumption curve will normally lie to one side or the other of $OTT'$ beyond $T$. If the income-elasticity of demand for $Y$ is greater than unity, and that for $X$ is less than unity, the income-consumption curve lies to the left of $TT'$ in the region $CTT'$; the ratio of $Y{:}X$ that would be purchased at initial prices is higher after the increase in income. When the growth of income thus raises the demand for importables $Y$ in greater proportion than it increases the demand for exportables $X$, the consumption effect can be termed "export-biased"—that is, on the side of demand, development is biased against exportables. A consumption effect which is export-biased will require a relative increase in the supply of exports to pay for the greater proportional share of importables in total consumption. At this point, Professor Johnson's terminology of "pro-trade-bias" is useful in avoiding any confusion.

If, however, the income-elasticity of demand for $Y$ is less than unity, and that for $X$ is greater than unity, the income-consumption curve lies to the right of $TT'$ in the region $C'TT'$; the ratio of $Y{:}X$ that would be purchased at initial prices is lower after the increase in income. When the growth of income thus raises the demand for importables Y in lesser proportion than it increases the demand for exportables X, the consumption effect can be termed "import-biased"—that is, on the side of demand, development is biased against imports.

The two possible consumption effects that remain may be described as "ultra-export-biased" when the demand for exportables falls absolutely as income rises, and "ultra-import-biased" when the demand for importables falls absolutely as income rises. These are, however, exceptional cases involving inferior goods, a situation of falling per capita income with population growth, or the possible effects of income redistribution; for simplicity, we exclude them from further consideration.

We must, however, allow for the possibility that development will alter the relative demand for commodities not only because income increases, but also because the preference system will be modified if tastes change or income is redistributed. Instead of considering an income-consumption line as based on an unchanged preference system, we must then refer to a "demand expansion line,"[22] which shows the combined result of changes in income and preferences on the relative demand for the commodities, at constant prices. If the particular demand expansion depends only on the income elasticity of demand—that is, tastes and the income distribution do not change—the demand expansion line corresponds to an income-consumption line. If, however, the different types of factor growth or technical change also result in different patterns of demand, the demand expansion line will diverge from a given income-consumption line. A change in tastes in favor of commodity X, for example, or a redistribu-

[22] Cf. Corden, op. cit., p. 225.

tion of income in favor of that factor which has higher average and marginal propensities to consume $X$ than has the other factor, would cause the demand expansion line in Fig. 5 to be to the right of a given income-consumption curve. Conversely, changes in tastes and income distribution which would favor the consumption of $Y$ as compared with $X$ would cause the demand expansion line to be to the left of a given income-consumption curve.

11.    We can now proceed to incorporate the various production and consumption effects into the offer curve analysis of traditional trade theory. Having considered separately the production and consumption shifts associated with development, we can next combine the various production and consumption effects to determine their over-all bias and their total effect on the developing country's demand for imports. To derive this total effect, we must weigh the change in the domestic supply of importables, as given by the production effect, against the change in demand for importables, as given by the consumption effect.[23] In accordance with the type and degree of over-all bias, the developing country's offer curve will then shift, and a new international trade equilibrium will tend to result. The type of over-all bias will determine the direction of movement of the offer curve, while the extent of the shift in the offer curve will depend on the degree of the over-all bias and on the rate of growth in total production. Once the offer curve shifts, we can then note the change in the volume of trade and the terms of trade.

The over-all bias in the development of country $E$ is neu-

[23] In the case of complete specialization in production, however, the over-all bias depends only on the consumption effect as national output expands, since the country itself produces none of the commodity which it imports.

tral if the biases on both the production and consumption sides are neutral.[24] In this case, the country's demand for importables and its supply of exports increase proportionately to the expansion in total output. But since imports are equivalent to the excess of consumption over the domestic production of importables, the domestic supply of importables is necessarily a smaller fraction of total output than is consumption of imports of total consumption; under conditions of neutral total bias, the difference between the demand for and the home supply of importables at constant prices must therefore become larger. Country $E$'s offer curve is then displaced from $OE$ to, say, $OE_N$ in Fig. 3, indicating that at each level of the terms of trade the demand for imports by $E$ and the supply of exports from $E$ are greater than before $E$'s production frontier shifted outwards. Assuming for simplicity no development in country $G$, and hence no change in $G$'s

[24] The degree of bias in the production effect can be measured by the excess over unity of the output-elasticity of the domestic production of importables; the degree of bias in the consumption effect, by the excess over unity of the output-elasticity of demand for importables. On both the production and consumption sides, the degrees of bias will be positive for export-bias and negative for import-bias. The total effect is export-biased, neutral, or import-biased according as $b_c + \frac{P}{C} b_p \gtrless 0$, where $b_c$ is the degree of bias in consumption, $b_p$ is the degree of bias in production, $P$ is the domestic production of importables, and $C$ represents consumption of importables. Johnson, International Trade and Economic Growth, op. cit., p. 78.

It may be noted, however, that the over-all bias will not be neutral even though production is export-biased and consumption is import-biased, and the biases are of the same degree. This is because the consumption of imports initially represents an excess demand over the domestic supply of importables, so that to have neutrality on balance the import-bias in consumption must be offset by a sufficiently greater opposite bias in production. If the degree of bias in the production change is not sufficiently greater than the degree of bias on the side of consumption, the consumption bias will dominate on balance.

offer curve, the new position of trade equilibrium is at $C'$. In this case, the volume of trade has expanded, and the commodity terms of trade have deteriorated for country $E$.

If both the production effect and the consumption effect are export-biased, the total effect is also export-biased. Or if the production effect is neutral, but the consumption effect is export-biased, the total effect will be export-biased. The total effect will also be export-biased if the production effect is export-biased and the consumption effect is neutral. The demand for imports and supply of exports then increase more than proportionately to the growth of total output. $E$'s offer curve shifts from $OE$ to, say, $OE_x$ in Fig. 3, and the new equilibrium is at $C''$. The volume of trade expands, and the terms of trade worsen for country $E$. Given the same rate of growth in total production, the increase in the volume of trade and the deterioration in the terms of trade are greater in this case than when the total bias was neutral.

If the consumption effect is import-biased, and the production effect is neutral or import-biased, the total effect is import-biased or possibly ultra-import-biased, depending on the degrees of bias in production and consumption. Or if there is import-bias in production, and a neutral consumption effect, the total effect will again be import-biased or possibly ultra-import-biased. When production is not sufficiently import-biased to more than offset the greater absolute demand for imports, the total effect will be simply import-biased. The demand for imports and the supply of exports then increase less than proportionately to total output. The offer curve shifts to the right of $OE$, but not as far as $OE_N$ to, say, $OE_M$. Given the unchanged offer curve for $G$, the absolutely greater demand for imports tends to worsen $E$'s terms of trade, although for the same rate of growth in total output the deterioration will now be less than in the neutral case of an increased demand for imports proportional to output.

If the import bias in production is sufficient to meet not only the increased absolute demand for importables that results from the output expansion but also some of the original demand for imports, the total effect will be ultra-import-biased. The absolute demand for imports and the supply of exports will be diminished; the offer curve will then shift to the left of $OE$ to, say, $OE_{UM}$. At the new equilibrium position $C'''$, the volume of trade is less than before development occurred, and the terms of trade are improved for country $E$.

If there is an ultra-import-bias on the production side, the total effect must also be ultra-import-biased; for the ultra-import-bias in production means that the domestic output of importables will increase more than total output, so that the demand for imports and the supply of exports fall absolutely.

If, however, there is an ultra-export-bias in production, there cannot be an over-all ultra-import-bias because the domestic output of importables falls absolutely. Depending on the consumption effect, the total effect may be ultra-export-biased, export-biased, or import-biased. If it is ultra-export-biased, the absolute demand for imports increases by more than the entire increase in national income, and the supply of exports increases more than in even the case of export-bias. Given the same rate of growth in total output, the offer curve would thus shift from $OE$ to the right beyond $OE_X$. The volume of trade would then be larger, and the deterioration in country $E$'s terms of trade would be greater than in the case of an over-all export-bias.

The variety of over-all biases that may result from different combinations of production and consumption effects can be summarized as follows, where the different total effects are indicated within the table:[25]

[25] Cf. Black and Streeten, *op. cit.*, p. 308.

| Type of Consumption Effect | Type of Production Effect | | | | |
|---|---|---|---|---|---|
| | N | X | M | UM | UX |
| N | N | X | M or UM | UM | X or UX |
| X | X | X | Not UX | UM | X or UX |
| M | M or UM | Not UX | M or UM | UM | Not UM |

| | |
|---|---|
| N = neutral | UM = ultra-import-bias |
| X = export-bias | UX = ultra-export-bias |
| M = import-bias | |

**12.** Although the foregoing model could be embellished at many points, especially by incorporating additional countries or commodities or factors, we are concerned here with only the central logic of how the structure of comparative costs may change in the course of development. Tedious as it may have been to work through the variety of possible cases, and even though we have not ventured beyond the method of comparative statics, our analysis in this chapter certainly indicates that changes in comparative costs can be readily incorporated into traditional trade theory.

More than that, the analysis provides a set of questions to ask in considering a range of international development problems. The analysis may be used to explain historical relationships between the spread of development in the international economy and changes in the volume and pattern of trade. And it may offer insights into whether the future spread of industrialization will lead to an increase or decline in world trade. As has already been done, some elements of the analysis may also be related to the adjustments required for the maintenance of international equilibrium between manufacturing and primary-producing countries,[26] or the analysis

[26] Johnson, *International Trade and Economic Growth, op. cit.,* chap. III.

may be applied to the problem of the effects of a population increase on a country's foreign trade.[27] Instead of pursuing these specific applications, we shall find it more useful in subsequent chapters to use this analysis in a more general fashion to help sort out the forces governing secular movements in the terms of trade, the developmental effects of foreign investment, and the influences of commercial policy on a country's development.

[27] W. M. Corden, "The Economic Limits to Population Increase," *Economic Record*, November, 1955, pp. 242-260.

# 3   *Terms of Trade*

**1.**  Despite all the ambiguities obscuring their use, the terms of trade still receive considerable attention in discussions of economic development. This is so not only because the terms of trade have sizeable quantitative significance for most poor countries, but also because they are a convenient indication of the net result of many diverse forces, and may have important welfare implications. We shall therefore analyze in this chapter the determinants of secular changes in the terms of trade and attempt to assess the influence of these changes on the development of a poor country.[1]

**2.**  Several different concepts of the terms of trade may be distinguished: the gross barter, net barter or commodity, income, single-factoral, double-factoral, real cost, and utility

---

[1] The short-run problem of fluctuations in the terms of trade is referred to in Chapter 7, sections 9 and 10.

terms of trade.[2] These several concepts fall into three groups:
(1) those that relate to the ratio of exchange between commodities—the gross barter, net barter, and income terms of
trade; (2) those that relate to the interchange between productive resources—the single-factoral and double-factoral
terms of trade; and (3) those that interpret the gains from
trade in terms of utility analysis—the real cost and utility
terms of trade.

In considering the barter terms of trade, Taussig introduced the distinction between "net" and "gross" barter
terms.[3] The commodity or net barter terms of trade $(N)$ are
expressed as $N = P_x/P_m$, where $P_x$ and $P_m$ are price index
numbers of exports and imports, respectively. A rise in $N$
indicates that a larger volume of imports could be received,
on the basis of price relations only, in exchange for a given
volume of exports. According to Taussig, however, the net
barter terms are relevant only when nothing enters into the
trade between countries except sales and purchases of mer-
chandise.

If the balance of payments includes unilateral payments,
so that there is an excess in money value of either exports or
imports, then the relevant concept is the gross barter terms
$(G)$. This measures the rate of exchange between the whole
of a country's physical imports as compared with the whole
of its exports, and is expressed as $G = Q_m/Q_x$, where $Q_m$ and

[2] Cf. Jacob Viner, *Studies in the Theory of International Trade,*
Harper & Brothers, 1937, pp. 558-564; W. W. Rostow, "The Terms of
Trade in Theory and Practice," *Economic History Review,* Second
Series, vol. III, No. 1, 1950, pp. 1-20; R. G. D. Allen and J. E. Ely,
eds., *International Trade Statistics,* John Wiley & Sons, 1953, pp. 207-
209; Gottfried Haberler, *A Survey of International Trade Theory,* International Finance Section, Princeton University, revised edition,
1961, pp. 24-29.

[3] F. W. Taussig, *International Trade,* Macmillan & Co., 1927, pp.
113, 117, 248-249.

$Q_x$ are volume index numbers for imports and exports, respectively. A rise in $G$ represents a "favorable" change in the sense that more imports are received for a given volume of exports than in the base year. Since $G = N$ only if the value of imports and value of exports are equal,[4] $G$ and $N$ diverge when there are unilateral transactions. But one must distinguish among the different types of unilateral transactions that cause changes in $G$. It is then more meaningful to consider the significance of various unilateral transactions directly, instead of incorporating them in the terms of trade index.[5]

Since it is especially important for a poor country to take changes in its volume of exports into account, we may want to correct the movements in $N$ for changes in export volume. The income terms of trade $(I)$ do this, and are expressed as $I = N \cdot Q_x$, where $Q_x$ is the export volume index.[6] A rise in $I$ indicates that the country can obtain a larger volume of imports from the sale of its exports; its "capacity to import" —based on exports—has increased. The export-based capacity to import should be distinguished, of course, from the total capacity to import, which depends not only on exports but also capital inflow and other invisible exchange receipts. Nor should a change in the income terms of trade be interpreted

[4] If $V_m$ and $V_x$ are index numbers of values of imports and exports, respectively, $\dfrac{G}{N} = \dfrac{Q_m}{Q_x} \cdot \dfrac{P_m}{P_x} = \dfrac{V_m}{V_x}.$

[5] Cf. Gottfried Haberler, *The Theory of International Trade*, William Hodge & Co., 1936, pp. 164-165; Viner, *op. cit.*, p. 563; Erick Schiff, "Direct Investments, Terms of Trade, and Balance of Payments," *Quarterly Journal of Economics*, February, 1942, pp. 310-316.

[6] G. S. Dorrance, "The Income Terms of Trade," *Review of Economic Studies*, 1948-49, pp. 50-56. The income terms of trade have also been referred to as "the export gain from trade"; A. H. Imlah, "The Terms of Trade of the United Kingdom, 1798-1913," *Journal of Economic History*, November, 1950, p. 176.

as a measure of the gain from trade or an indicator of welfare; it should be used simply as a measure of the quantity of imports bought by exports.

It is significant that, according to the direction and magnitude of the changes in $P_x$ and $Q_x$, the changes in $I$ and $N$ may be in opposite directions. If, for example, with unchanged import prices, export prices have fallen, but export quantities $(Q_x)$ have increased by a greater percentage than the decrease in $P_x$, the income terms of trade will have improved despite a deterioration in the commodity terms of trade.

Changes in productivity are obviously also of prime significance in considering development, and one may therefore want to refer to the factoral terms of trade. The single-factoral terms $(S)$ correct the commodity terms for changes in productivity in producing exports, and may be expressed as $S = N \cdot Z_x$, where $Z_x$ is an export productivity index. A rise in $S$ is a favorable movement in the sense that a greater quantity of imports can be obtained per unit of factor-input used in the production of exportables.

If $N$ is corrected for changes in productivity in producing imports as well as exports, the result is the double-factoral terms of trade *(D)*, expressed as $D = N \cdot Z_x/Z_m$, where $Z_m$ is an import productivity index. A rise in $D$ shows that one unit of home factors embodied in exports now exchanges for more units of the foreign factors embodied in imports. $D$ will diverge from $S$ when there is a change in the factor cost of producing imports, but this has no welfare significance for the importing country, even though it indicates a change in productivity in the other country from which commodities are imported. What matters to the importing country is whether it receives more goods per unit of its "exported factor-input" (an improvement in $S$)—not whether these imports contain more or less foreign inputs than before.

It may also be noted that $N$ will equal $D$ when constant returns to scale prevail, and there are no historical changes in costs and no transport costs. But if costs are variable with respect to output or time, or there are transport costs, $N$ and $D$ will diverge. Although this divergence is analytically significant, it is difficult to measure as long as a productivity index remains an elusive concept. In the offer curve analysis of the preceding chapter, the terms of trade as determined at the positions of equilibrium in Fig. 3 are the commodity terms. If, however, we had followed Marshall, and considered on each axis "representative bundles" or "bales" of commodities that contained a constant quantity of "productive resources," the terms of trade would have been the double-factoral terms.

Proceeding more directly to the level of welfare analysis, we may define in utility terms the total amount of gain from trade as the excess of the total utility accruing from imports over the total sacrifice of utility involved in the surrender of exports.[7] To consider the amount of disutility involved in the production of exports, we may correct the single-factoral terms of trade index by multiplying $S$ by the reciprocal of an index of the amount of disutility per unit of productive resources used in producing exports.[8] The resultant index would be a real cost terms of trade index ($R$). If $R$ rises as a result of a change in the methods of producing exports, or a change in the factor proportions used in exports, this would indicate that the amount of imports obtained per unit of real cost was greater.

On the side of demand, we may want to allow for changes in the relative desirability of the imports and the domestic commodities whose home consumption is foregone because

[7] Viner, *op. cit.*, p. 557.
[8] *Ibid.*, p. 559.

of the use of resources in export production. It is then necessary to incorporate into R an index of the relative average utility per unit of imports and of foregone domestic commodities. The resultant index is the utility terms of trade (U), equal to R multiplied by an index of the relative utility of imports and foregone commodities.[9]

The difficulty with the use of R and U is, of course, that of calculating the disutility involved in export production, or the relative average utility of various commodities. The welfare significance of changes in the terms of trade must therefore be considered only indirectly, along the lines suggested below in section 5, and not directly through any measurement of R or U.

Having minimized the significance of changes in G, D, R, and U, we are thus left with N, S, and I as the most relevant concepts of the terms of trade for poor countries. Movements in N, S, and I may diverge, however, and these divergences are not merely technical but are due to fundamentally different circumstances. Accordingly, they have different consequences for the country's development. To assess the significance for a poor country of an alteration in its commodity terms of trade—the most frequently cited change—we must therefore analyze the determinants of this change and also the attendant movements in the income and single-factoral terms of trade.

3.  Over the short period, the terms of trade may vary as a consequence of changes in commercial policy, exchange rate variations, unilateral transfer payments, or cyclical fluctuations. Over the long period, which is relevant for development problems, the determinants of changes in the terms of trade are associated with structural variations in production and consumption that may be examined in the light of the

[9] *Ibid.*, pp. 560-561.

offer curve analysis of the preceding chapter. As already noted, the shifts in the offer curves will cause movements in the terms of trade, and the various possible shifts in the offer curves can be attributed, in turn, to different types of development.[10]

Assuming that development occurs only in country $E$, so that $G$'s offer curve remains fixed while $E$'s offer curve shifts, we can summarize the various changes in $E$'s commodity terms of trade, according to the different total biases in development, as follows:

| Type of Total Bias in Development | Direction of Change in Commodity Terms of Trade |
|:---:|:---:|
| $N$ | $(-)$ |
| $X$ | $(-)$ |
| $M$ | $(-)$ |
| $UM$ | $(+)$ |
| $UX$ | $(-)$ |

| | |
|---|---|
| $N$ = neutral | $(-)$ = deterioration |
| $X$ = export-bias | $(+)$ = improvement |
| $M$ = import-bias | |
| $UM$ = ultra-import-bias | |
| $UX$ = ultra-export-bias | |

When development occurs only in $E$, and $G$'s offer curve is not infinitely elastic, the terms of trade for $E$ deteriorate for each type of total bias except an ultra-import bias. As in-

[10] For other analyses of the effects on international trade of shifts in reciprocal demand schedules of different elasticities, see Murray C. Kemp, "The Relation between Changes in International Demand and the Terms of Trade," *Econometrica*, January, 1956, pp. 41-46; W. R. Allen, "The Effects on Trade of Shifting Reciprocal Demand Schedules," *American Economic Review*, March, 1952, pp. 135-140.

dicated previously (Fig. 3), the deterioration for a given increase in total output is least, however, when there is an import-bias, and the demand for imports increases less than proportionately to the expansion in total output. The deterioration is greatest when there is an ultra-export-bias, and the absolute demand for imports increases more than total output. In general, the rate of deterioration in $E$'s commodity terms of trade will be greater under the following conditions: the larger is the degree of export-bias on balance in $E$; the higher is the rate of increase in $E$'s total output; the lower is $E$'s elasticity of demand for $G$'s goods; and the lower is $G$'s elasticity of demand for imports from $E$.

4.   When development occurs in both $E$ and $G$, the movement of the terms of trade depends on the rate of increase in each country's demand for imports from the other country— in other words, on the relative shifts of the offer curves as determined by the type of total bias and the rate of development in each country.

If the total bias in the development of each country is neutral, each country's offer curve shifts outwards, with the extent of the shift depending on the rate of development. The terms of trade will therefore deteriorate for the country that has the higher rate of development.

If in each country development is ultra-export-biased, or export-biased, or import-biased, each country's offer curve again shifts outwards. The terms of trade would then remain constant only if the types and degrees of bias and rates of development had the same total effect on the growth of demand for imports in each country. In the general case, the terms of trade deteriorate for that country which has the greater rate of growth of demand for imports as determined by its degree of bias, as well as rate of development.

If the over-all effects are export-biased in $E$, but import-biased in $G$, then, assuming the rate of development is the same in each country, the terms of trade will deteriorate for $E$. If, however, the rate of development in $E$ is sufficiently lower than in $G$, the terms of trade will improve for $E$, even though its development is export-biased.

The relative rates of development in the two countries may, in many cases, be significant in offsetting the different degrees or types of bias. If, however, the development is ultra-import-biased in only one of the countries, the terms of trade will improve for that country regardless of the type of bias in the other country and the relative rates of development.

From these diverse cases it is apparent that there is no invariant relationship between a country's development and movements in its commodity terms of trade. Depending on the type and degree of bias and the rate of development in each country, the terms of trade may either improve or deteriorate.

**5.** The connection between changes in the terms of trade and economic welfare is an especially difficult problem: in what sense may a movement in a country's terms of trade be accepted as an index of the trend in economic welfare? Considerable care must be exercised to avoid the fallacy of equating a change in any of the various terms of trade with a variation in the amount or even direction of change in the gains from trade. Such an equation cannot be adduced until we determine the underlying forces associated with the change in the terms of trade, and until we connect the terms of trade, relating to a unit of trade, with the volume of trade.

The welfare implications of a change in the commodity terms of trade are most directly seen in the effect on real national income. When a country's commodity terms of trade improve, its real income rises faster than output, since the purchasing power of a unit of its exports rises. This increase in real income will supplement the benefit that the country derives from its own development.[11] If, however, a country experiences a deterioration in its terms of trade as it develops, part of the benefit from an expansion in its own output is thereby cancelled.

Insofar as a slower rate of development might allow a country's commodity terms of trade to improve, whereas a higher rate would cause a deterioration, it is possible that the gain from the improvement in the terms of trade might be more than sufficient to compensate for the output foregone by the slower expansion in home output. In the case of an ultra-import-bias, however, a lower rate of development would not tend to augment the improvement in the commodity terms of trade. On the contrary, unlike the other cases, a higher rate of development in this situation will not only increase domestic output further, but will also cause a greater improvement in the commodity terms of trade.

As an extreme case, it is possible that the type and rate of development may cause so severe a deterioration in the terms of trade that the gain from the growth in output is more than offset by the loss from adverse terms of trade. This theoretical possibility has been demonstrated by Bhagwati, who describes it as a case of "immiserizing growth."[12] For example,

[11] An improvement in the commodity terms of trade might facilitate an expansion in domestic output by permitting the release of resources from export production to domestic production. If the improvement is due to a rise in export prices, this may contribute to an increase in public saving through export taxes, income taxes, or a rise in the profits of governmental marketing boards.

[12] Jagdish Bhagwati, "Immiserizing Growth: A Geometrical Note," *Review of Economic Studies*, June, 1958, pp. 201-205; "International Trade and Economic Expansion," *American Economic Review*, Decem-

an increase in factor supply or technical progress would raise
real income by the amount of the change in output at constant prices, but if the factor accumulation or "factor-saving"
is so export-biased that the terms of trade worsen, the negative income effect of the actual deterioration in the terms of
trade may then be greater than the positive effect of the expansion in ouput.

Although analytically interesting, the practical bearing of
this possibility is very limited. The conditions necessary for
immiserization to result are highly restrictive. In the case of
incomplete specialization, the possibility can arise only if the
increased quantity of the factor is allocated to export industries, and either the foreign demand for the growing country's exports is inelastic or the country's expansion actually
reduces the domestic production of importables.[13] But if external demand is so unfavorable, then additional resources
will not flow into the export sector when the situation is such
that the very growth of factor supplies may actually have to
be induced by the existence of profitable openings for the
employment of these additional factors. Moreover, even if
there is an autonomous increase in factors, there is still no

---

ber, 1958, pp. 941-953; "Growth, Terms of Trade and Comparative
Advantage," *Economia Internazionale*, August, 1959, pp. 395-398.

Some classical and neoclassical economists also recognized this possibility when they considered the impact of technological change upon
the terms of trade. Cf. J. S. Mill, *Principles of Political Economy*,
Longmans, Green & Co., 1848, Book III, chap. XVIII, sec. 5; C. F.
Bastable, *The Theory of International Trade*, fourth edition, Macmillan
& Co., 1903, appendix C, pp. 185-187; F. Y. Edgeworth, "The Theory
of International Values, I," *Economic Journal*, March, 1894, pp. 40-42.

[13] Bhagwati, "International Trade and Economic Expansion," *op.
cit.*, pp. 949-952. In the case of complete specialization, it is necessary
that both the foreign demand for exports and the domestic demand for
imports be inelastic. This proposition is demonstrated by Bhagwati
and Johnson, *op. cit.*, pp. 80-81.

basis for "immiserizing growth," inasmuch as increments in factor supplies are as a rule mobile and the economy has some capacity for transforming its structure of output. Factor increments, therefore, need not flow into the export sector in accordance with a predetermined pattern of production.[14] To be valid, the "immiserizing growth" argument depends on highly restrictive conditions with respect to elasticities of demand and supply—conditions which are unlikely to apply when an economy has some flexibility in its structure of output and some capacity for adapting to changed circumstances. It should also be realized that, even if the necessary conditions do exist, the country can still institute offsetting policies and impose taxes on its trade sufficient to gain some of the benefits of the expanded production.[15]

If we examine the welfare implications of a change in the terms of trade more broadly, we can readily identify circumstances under which a country need not be worse off, even though its commodity terms deteriorate. When the deterioration results from a shift only in the foreign offer curve, with the country's own offer curve unchanged, the resultant deterioration in the country's terms of trade is clearly unfavorable. If, however, the domestic offer curve also shifts, then it is necessary to consider the causes of this shift and also the possible changes in the factoral and income terms of trade.

For instance, development may occur in both countries $E$ and $G$, but the rate of growth of demand for imports may be greater in $E$ than in $G$, so that $E$'s commodity terms of trade

[14] Cf. Ragnar Nurkse, *Patterns of Trade and Development,* Wicksell Lectures, Almquist & Wiksell, 1959, pp. 56, 58-59 (reprinted in *Equilibrium and Growth in the World Economy. Economic Essays by Ragnar Nurkse,* Harvard University Press, 1961, pp. 332-334).

[15] Cf. R. A. Mundell, "The Pure Theory of International Trade," *American Economic Review,* March, 1960, p. 85.

deteriorate. Nonetheless, $E$ may still be better off than before if the deterioration in its commodity terms is due to export-biased increases in productivity. In this case the single-factoral terms of trade improve, and the deterioration in the commodity terms is only a reflection of the increased productivity in $E$'s export industries. As long as productivity in $E$'s export sector is rising faster than the prices of its exports are falling, its real income rises despite the deterioration in its commodity terms of trade. If the prices of exports in terms of imports fall by a smaller percentage than the percentage increase in productivity, the country clearly benefits from its ability to obtain a greater quantity of imports per unit of factors embodied in its exports.

Classical and neoclassical economists recognized this possibility and attempted to go behind the quantities of exports and imports to consider what, as Pigou remarked, "underlie the exports, namely a given quantity of labor and service of capital." It may then be that although the commodity terms of trade deteriorate when the production costs of exports fall, the country may receive more imports than previously for what "underlies its exports." A divergence between the commodity terms and the factoral terms was meant to be avoided by J. S. Mill's conception of "cost," Bastable's "unit of productive power," and Marshall's "representative bales of commodities," each of which contains a constant quantity of "productive resources." But as already noted, if we allow for more than two commodities, transportation costs, or variable costs of production, the commodity terms and the factoral terms of trade may diverge.

It is also relevant that even if productivity is not rising in the export sector, and the commodity terms of trade are deteriorating, it is still possible for the real income of the factors to rise. This may occur under conditions of a "dual economy" in which factors are initially employed in the backward domestic sector with lower productivity than exists in the advanced export sector. If export production should then expand and attract these factors into the export sector, the factors will gain to the extent that their marginal productivity in the export sector remains above their marginal productivity in the sector from which they withdraw. At the same time, the real prices of export products may be falling, and the commodity terms of trade may be worsening.[16]

A high degree of export-bias on the side of consumption may also cause a deterioration in $E$'s commodity terms of trade. But if this export-bias is due to a change in tastes or a redistribution of income, it is difficult to reach any welfare conclusion. For the intervening change in the preference system makes it impossible to conclude that the later result is inferior to the previous situation merely because the commodity terms have deteriorated. If the terms worsen because demand increases for imports, it may not be true that from the criterion of "utility" a loss is incurred. What must be considered is not the utility of the import alone, but also its utility relative to that of the domestic commodities whose domestic consumption is precluded by allocation of resources to production for export. Were it measurable, the utility terms of trade index would be appropriate for this type of change.

We should also realize that it is possible for the country's income terms of trade to improve at the same time as its commodity terms deteriorate. If the foreign offer curve is elastic,[17] or if the foreign offer curve shifts out sufficiently, the volume of exports may increase enough to improve the

[16] Cf. Theodore Morgan, "The Long-Run Terms of Trade Between Agriculture and Manufacturing," *Economic Development and Cultural Change*, October, 1959, pp. 17-18.

[17] When the offer curve is of the normal "elastic" sort, more imports are demanded and more exports are supplied as the price of imports falls.

income terms of trade despite the deterioration in the commodity terms. The country's capacity to import is then greater, and this can be of decided significance for a developing country. Such an improvement in the capacity to import is especially important for a poor country which has a high average propensity to import. It would, of course, be even better for the country if its greater volume of exports could be traded at unchanged prices. But this involves a comparison with a hypothetical situation, whereas the relevant consideration is the effect of the actual change between the previous and present situations.

In contrast, a country's development program may be handicapped, despite an improvement in its commodity terms, if its capacity to import is reduced because of a fall in the volume of exports that is not offset sufficiently by the improved commodity terms. If, for example, a country's development is ultra-import-biased so that its commodity terms improve, but the foreign offer curve is not inelastic, or it shifts inwards relatively more than does the domestic offer curve, the country's income terms will deteriorate. Regardless of its more favorable commodity terms, the country's capacity to import is then reduced, and this may hamper the country's developmental efforts if the growth in output has not been sufficiently import-saving.

These examples illustrate that the mere knowledge of a change in the commodity terms of trade does not in itself allow a firm conclusion as to the effect on the country's economic welfare. It is essential to proceed beyond this superficial level and consider whether the change has been caused by a shift only in the foreign offer curve or by a shift in the domestic offer curve. If by the latter, then the cause of the shift becomes relevant and may deserve more emphasis than the fact of the change itself. Attention to the underlying cause is especially needed for recognizing movements in the single-factoral terms as well as commodity terms of trade, and for determining possible changes in the pattern of demand. Finally, changes in the volume of trade must always be considered along with price variations.

**6.** With the foregoing general considerations in mind, we may now examine the validity of the often-repeated contention that the poor countries have suffered a secular deterioration in their commodity terms of trade.[18] On the basis of inferences from the United Kingdom's commodity terms of trade, proponents of this view claim that "from the latter part of the nineteenth century to the eve of the second world war . . . there was a secular downward trend in the prices of primary goods relative to the prices of manufactured goods. On an average, a given quantity of primary exports would pay, at the end of this period, for only 60 percent of the quantity of manufactured goods which it could buy at the beginning of the period."[19]

[18] This allegation appears in several reports of the United Nations and in various writings by Raúl Prebisch, Hans Singer, W. A. Lewis, and Gunnar Myrdal, among others. It is noteworthy that this view is completely at variance with that commonly held by classical economists who believed that the operation of diminishing returns in primary production would cause the prices of primary products to rise relatively to prices of manufactures. Keynes restated the classical view in his "Reply to Sir William Beveridge," *Economic Journal*, December, 1923, pp. 476-488; also, D. H. Robertson, *A Study of Industrial Fluctuation*, P. S. King & Son, Ltd., 1915, p. 169.  *Colin Clark*

[19] United Nations, Department of Economic Affairs, *Relative Prices of Exports and Imports of Underdeveloped Countries*, 1949, p. 72. The indices used are based on Werner Schlote, *Entwicklung und Strukturwandlungen des englischen Aussenhandels von 1700 bis zur Gegenwart*, Probleme der Weltwirtschaft, No. 62, Jena, 1938. Other indices constructed by Professors Imlah and Kindleberger do not show as marked an improvement for Britain as do Schlote's; A. H. Imlah, *Eco-*

The causes of this deterioration are supposedly associated with differences in the distribution of the gains from increased productivity, diverse cyclical movements of primary product and industrial prices, and disparities in the rates of increase in demand for imports between the industrial and primary producing countries. Since technical progress has been greater in industry than in the primary production of poor countries, it is suggested that if prices had been reduced in proportion to increasing productivity, the reduction should then have been less for primary products than for manufactures, so that as the disparity between productivities increased, the price relationship between the two should have improved in favor of the poor countries. It is alleged, however, that the opposite occurred: in respect to manufactured commodities produced in more developed countries, it is contended that the gains from increased productivity have been distributed in the form of higher wages and profits rather than lower prices, whereas in the case of food and raw material production in the underdeveloped countries the gains in productivity, although smaller, have been distributed in the form of price reductions.[20]

---

*nomic Elements in the Pax Britannica,* Harvard University Press, 1958, chap. IV, Table 8; C. P. Kindleberger, *The Terms of Trade, A European Case Study,* John Wiley & Sons, 1956, pp. 53 ff.

W. A. Lewis' consideration of the prices of primary products and manufactures also relies heavily on Schlote's data; Lewis, "World Production, Prices and Trade, 1870-1960," *Manchester School of Economic and Social Studies,* May, 1952, Table II.

[20] United Nations, Department of Economic Affairs, *The Economic Development of Latin America and Its Principal Problems,* 1950, pp. 8-14; *Relative Prices of Exports and Imports of Underdeveloped Countries, op. cit.,* pp. 13-24, 126; H. W. Singer, "The Distribution of Gains Between Investing and Borrowing Countries," *American Economic Review, Papers and Proceedings,* May, 1950, pp. 477-479; W. A. Lewis, "Economic Development with Unlimited Supplies of

This contrasting behavior of prices in industrial and primary producing countries is also attributed to the different movements of primary product prices and industrial prices over successive business cycles and to the greater number of monopoly elements in industrial markets.[21] According to this reasoning, the prices of primary products have risen sharply in prosperous periods, but have subsequently lost their gain in the downswing of the trade cycle. In contrast, it is asserted that although manufacturing prices have risen less in the upswing, they have not fallen as far in depression as they have risen in prosperity, because of the rigidity of industrial wages and price inflexibility in the more monopolistic industrial markets. It is therefore concluded that over successive cycles the gap between the prices of the two groups of commodities has widened, and the primary producing areas have suffered an unfavorable movement in their terms of trade.

Proponents of the secular deterioration hypothesis also argue that the differential price movements between poor and rich countries have been accentuated by a relative decrease in the demand for primary products and a relative increase in the demand for industrial products. This is attributed to the operation of Engel's law, and also in the case of raw materials to technical progress in manufacturing, which reduces the amount of raw materials used per unit of output.[22] The low income elasticity of demand and the struc-

Labour," *Manchester School of Economic and Social Studies,* May, 1954, pp. 183-184; F. Mehta, "The Effects of Adverse Income Terms of Trade on the Secular Growth of Underdeveloped Countries," *Indian Economic Journal,* July, 1956, pp. 9-21.

[21] *The Economic Development of Latin America and Its Principal Problems, op. cit.,* pp. 12-14.

[22] Singer, *op. cit.,* p. 479; Raúl Prebisch, "Commercial Policy in Underdeveloped Countries," *American Economic Review, Papers and Pro-*

tural changes result in a secular decline in the demand for primary products. In other words, the consumption effect of development in the poor country is export-biased (pro-trade-biased), whereas in the rich country it is import-biased (anti-trade-biased).

If the alleged secular deterioration in the terms of trade of poor countries were true it would mean that there has been an international transfer of income away from the poor countries, and this decrease in purchasing power would be significant in reducing their capacity for development. The thesis is, however, highly impressionistic and conjectural. When its content is examined more rigorously, the argument appears weak—both statistically and analytically.[23]

Although the relevant long-run data for individual poor countries are not readily available, the substitution of the "inverse" of the United Kingdom's terms of trade is merely an expedient and does not provide a sufficiently strong statistical foundation for any adequate generalization about the terms of trade of poor countries.[24] The import-price index is a mixed bag, concealing the heterogeneous price movements

---

*ceedings*, May, 1959, pp. 261-264. For a quantitative approach to some of the factors considered by Singer and Prebisch, see M. K. Atallah, *The Terms of Trade Between Agricultural and Industrial Products*, Netherlands Economic Institute, 1958.

[23] The most systematic appraisal of the argument has been presented by Gottfried Haberler, "Terms of Trade and Economic Development," Howard S. Ellis, ed., *Economic Development for Latin America*, St. Martin's Press, 1961, pp. 275-297. On the basis of several objections, largely similar to those we discuss below, Professor Haberler concludes that the reasons which have been advanced for the alleged trend are either fallacious or are entirely inadequate in their explanation.

[24] Cf. Morgan, *op. cit.*, pp. 6-17. From a consideration of six countries, Professor Morgan concludes that the highly diverse demand and supply experience for particular commodities of the different countries covered underlines the importance of not generalizing on the experience of other countries from that of the United Kingdom.

within and among the broad categories of foodstuffs, raw materials, and minerals. An aggregation of primary products cannot be representative of the wide variety of primary products exported by poor countries. Nor, of course, is it legitimate to identify all exporters of primary products as poor countries. Some primary producing countries are also importers of primary products. Moreover, the composition of exports from other industrial countries differs markedly from the United Kingdom's, making it unlikely that the United Kingdom's terms of trade can be truly representative for other industrial countries. It has been shown that the terms of trade for other industrial countries have behaved quite differently from those of the United Kingdom.[25]

Even if we were willing to use the British terms of trade as indirect evidence for the terms of trade between industrial and non-industrial countries, we should still have to be extremely skeptical about the reliability of the British data. Apart from all the statistical pitfalls connected with the construction of import and export price indices, there are strong biases in the United Kingdom series that make the terms of trade appear less favorable to poor countries than they actually were.[26] No allowance is made for changes in the quality of exports and imports; nor is there adequate coverage for the introduction of new commodities. Insofar as the improvements in quality and the introduction of new commodities have undoubtedly been more pronounced for industrial products than for primary products, a simple inversion of the United Kingdom's terms of trade would thus overstate any unfavorable movement for countries exporting

[25] Kindleberger, *op. cit.*, pp. 53 ff., 233.
[26] Cf. Morgan, *op. cit.*, pp. 4-6; R. E. Baldwin, "Secular Movements in the Terms of Trade," *American Economic Review, Papers and Proceedings*, May, 1955, pp. 267-268.

primary products to the United Kingdom and importing industrial products from it.

Furthermore, there is no allowance for the fact that transportation costs were falling, making it invalid to infer from the British data what the terms of trade were for the primary producing countries trading with Britain. If the recorded terms of international trade were corrected for the decline in transportation costs that occurred, the improvement in the United Kingdom's terms would appear substantially less. This is because British exports are valued at the port of exit, while the value of imports includes shipping costs. A large part of the decline in British import prices, however, was caused by the fall in ocean freights, and if Britain's export price index were corrected for transportation costs it would show a greater decline than does the recorded British export price index.[27] A proper consideration of transportation costs makes the terms of trade of primary producers appear less unfavorable.

These statistical imperfections do not allow much support for the hypothesis of a secular deterioration in the terms of trade for poor countries. It might even be maintained that their terms of trade improved because of quality improvements in their imports, access to a wider range of imports, and the great relative decline in transportation costs as compared with the prices of the commodities transported.

If the empirical evidence does not bear close scrutiny, still less does the analytical explanation. The validity of the ap-

[27] Statistical confirmation is given in L. Isserlis, "Tramp Shipping Cargoes and Freights," *Journal of Royal Statistical Society,* 1938, p. 122; Kindleberger, *op. cit.,* pp. 20-21, 336-339; C. M. Wright, "Convertibility and Triangular Trade as Safeguards against Economic Depression," *Economic Journal,* September, 1955, pp. 424-426; P. T. Ellsworth, "The Terms of Trade Between Primary Producing and Industrial Countries," *Inter-American Economic Affairs,* Summer, 1956, pp. 47-65.

peal to monopolistic elements in the industrial countries depends on the existence of monopoly in not only factor markets but also product markets,[28] so that the increasing productivity could be distributed in the form of rising money wages and profits, with stable or rising prices. It is an open question whether trade unions and firms actually possessed and exercised sufficient monopoly powers. But even if they did, the existence of such monopoly elements would at most explain movements in the absolute domestic price level and not changes in relative world prices of manufactures and primary products. World price levels depend on world conditions of supply and demand, and a country with a relatively high domestic price level may simply find itself priced out of international markets unless it makes some adjustment in its domestic prices or exchange rate.

Further, allowing for the neglected influence of transport costs over the cycle, we may also note many instances in which during a recession the prices of primary products declined in the United Kingdom, while actually rising at the ports of shipment in the primary producing countries.[29] Nor is the pre-1914 evidence on the purchasing power of primary products consistent with the cyclical explanation: Britain's terms of trade actually deteriorated during most depressions before 1914; Britain's food import prices fluctuated less in most trade cycles before 1914 than did British export prices; and a substantial number of primary products—especially foodstuffs—actually gained in purchasing power during many pre-1914 depressions.[30]

[28] Kindleberger, *op. cit.*, pp. 246-247, 304.
[29] Wright, *op. cit.*, pp. 425-426.
[30] K. Martin and F. G. Thackeray, "The Terms of Trade of Selected Countries, 1870-1938," *Bulletin of the Oxford University Institute of Statistics*, November, 1948, pp. 380-382; W. W. Rostow, "The Histori-

As for the appeal to disparities in the rates of increase in the demand for imports, this in itself cannot explain changes in relative prices. As has been stressed in the analysis of shifts in the offer curves, it is essential to consider also the rates of development and changes in supply conditions. For even though the percentage of expenditure on a given import might be a decreasing function of income, the absolute demand for the import may still be greater as development proceeds. In addition, shifts of the long-term supply elasticities within industrial countries may be such as to prevent the domestic output of importables from keeping up with demand, so that the import requirements may rise relatively to income growth in the industrial countries. It should also be remembered that Engel's law applies only to foodstuffs— not to industrial raw materials or minerals. And even if an income elasticity of demand of less than unity is accepted as reasonable for primary products, what is significant for a specific primary producing country is not this over-all elasticity but the expansion in demand for its own exports.

Finally, aside from its statistical and analytical weaknesses, the entire argument has been unduly restricted to only the commodity terms of trade. Also significant are changes in the income terms of trade and especially the single-factoral terms. It is clearly possible, as already noted, that a country's income terms and single-factoral terms might improve at the same time as its commodity terms deteriorate. Since the exports from poor countries have grown so considerably, and productivity in export production has increased, the income terms and single-factoral terms have undoubtedly improved for poor countries. This is actually implicit in the secular deterioration argument, insofar as it relies on productivity

cal Analysis of the Terms of Trade," *Economic History Review*, Second Series, vol. IV, No. 1, 1951, pp. 69-71.

increasing in both primary producing and industrial countries, but at a higher rate in the latter. Although their double-
factoral terms of trade may have deteriorated, this did not
affect the welfare of poor countries; they were better off
when their own single-factoral terms improved and they received more imports per unit of their "exported factors," regardless of whether the single-factoral terms also improved
for other countries exporting to them. Their capacity to import and their imports per unit of productive resources exported have increased—regardless of any changes in the
relative prices for their products.

The most favorable situation, of course, would be an improvement in the commodity terms of trade as well as in the
single-factoral and income terms. But the ruling conditions
may frequently be incompatible with such a simultaneous
improvement. Nonetheless, to look only at changes in the commodity terms is to neglect the favorable effects of the greater
capacity to import through improvement in the income terms
and the benefits from the improvement in the single-factoral
terms. When it is assessed within this wider analysis, a
change in the commodity terms of trade may prove to be of
small moment for a developing economy in comparison with
the more fundamental changes that have occurred at the
same time.

# 4    *External Balance*

**1.** Up to this point, in examining how the "real" forces of development manifest themselves internationally through changes in comparative advantages and variations in the terms of trade, we have assumed the existence of balance of payments equilibrium. We must now remove this assumption and consider one of the major problems confronting a poor country—the likelihood that an increase in its rate of development will place a severe strain on its balance of payments.

Of the various sources of balance of payments pressure, those associated with capital accumulation are of particular concern to a country undertaking a development program. Although cyclical instability, specific sectoral imbalances, or disproportionate rates of growth in the demand for exports and imports may all imperil a poor country's external balance,[1] a more prevalent cause of external imbalance is likely

[1] The view that balance of payments difficulties are due to specific output-input imbalances and disproportionalities which arise in the

to be the internal disequilibrium connected with a rise in the level of investment. In most development programs, a policy of accelerated capital formation entails a fundamental and chronic need for foreign exchange, and the country's rate of development becomes highly dependent on the ability to finance a large imbalance on current account. If to support its development program, a country has to run its international reserves down to a minimum, it will then be in a vulnerable position of not having adequate cover for shorter-run swings in its balance of payments. As its international reserves become deficient, the country finds itself under pressure to correct its external deficit. Out of consideration for the balance of payments, the development program may then have to be compromised. The necessity of avoiding a conflict between the objectives of accelerating capital formation and maintaining balance of payments equilibrium is therefore a primary restraint on the country's rate of development.

Several definitions of "balance of payments equilibrium" are possible, differing by the extent to which they incorporate normative elements. For present purposes we shall consider the balance of payments to be in equilibrium if over the relevant time period a country can meet its international payments out of its international receipts from current transactions and autonomous (ordinary or "acceptable") capital inflows, without being compelled to endure excessive unemployment or to restrict imports merely to avoid a deficit in the balance of payments. When a passive balance on current

course of growth is argued by A. O. Hirschman, *The Strategy of Economic Development,* Yale University Press, 1958, pp. 166-173.

For an attempt to attribute chronic disequilibrium in the balance of payments to a structural disequilibrium inherent in the process of development, see Celso Furtado, "The External Disequilibrium in the Underdeveloped Economies," *Indian Journal of Economics,* April, 1958, pp. 403-410.

account is not covered by an autonomous capital inflow, there is a need for induced (accommodating or "distress") capital transactions or a gold outflow. The country then suffers from an external disequilibrium which requires remedial action.

2.    As a basis for examining how the forces of development may disturb the balance of payments, we should first recall some fundamental relationships between national income and the balance of payments. Although national output, national income, and national expenditure are necessarily equal in a closed economy, they may diverge in an open economy.

National output $(O)$ is expressed as

$$O = C + I + X - M$$

where consumption $(C)$ and home investment $(I)$ include imported consumption and investment goods, $X$ represents value of all exports, and $M$ the value of all imports of goods and services in the balance of trade. If allowance is made for other items in the balance on current account, the national income $(Y)$ may differ from the national output according to

$$Y = O \pm R$$

where $+R$ represents the net payments received from abroad on account of interest and dividends from foreign investments, private unilateral transfers, and government aid $(-R$ would represent net payments made abroad on these items). The total domestic expenditure $(E)$, or the "total absorption" of consumption and investment goods, is

$$E = C + I = O - (X - M).$$

It follows that

$$X - M = O - E, \text{ and } (X - M) \pm R = Y - E.$$

From the last equation, it is clear that an external deficit consists in an excess of aggregate expenditure over real national income (output). If a country's level of national expenditure—or total absorption of resources—is larger than its home output plus the resources that it can import with an ordinary capital inflow, the consequence is a balance of payments deficit which must be financed by an accommodating capital inflow or gold outflow. In this situation the external imbalance is a direct manifestation of internal disequilibrium, and we may as readily speak of excess spending as of a balance of payments deficit, or as easily of "overabsorption" as of "overimporting."[2]

This essential relationship between internal imbalance and external imbalance is also apparent when the Harrod-Domar theory of equilibrium growth is applied to the balance of payments. Harrod writes his fundamental equation in the form $GC = s - b$, where: $G$, representing growth, is the increment of total production in any unit period expressed as a fraction of total production; $C$, capital, represents the investment of the period divided by the increment of production in the same period; $s$ is the fraction of income saved; and $b$ is the balance of trade expressed as a fraction of income.[3]

[2] This principle is fully elaborated by Ragnar Nurkse, "The Relation Between Home Investment and External Balance in the Light of British Experience, 1945-1955," *Review of Economics and Statistics,* May, 1956, pp. 137-147. The "absorption approach" to balance of payments policy was introduced by S. S. Alexander, "The Effects of a Devaluation on a Trade Balance," *International Monetary Fund Staff Papers,* April, 1952, pp. 263-278.

[3] R. F. Harrod, *Towards a Dynamic Economics,* Macmillan & Co. Ltd., 1948, p. 105. If allowance is made for other items in the current account, credits may be added to exports, and debits to imports, so that $b$ is then the balance on current account expressed as a fraction of income.

The equation can therefore be rewritten as

$$\frac{\Delta Y}{Y} \cdot \frac{I}{\Delta Y} = \frac{S}{Y} - \frac{(X - M)}{Y} \; ; \; \text{or} \; I + X = S + M.^4$$

Although this equation always holds true in the "realized" or *ex post* sense for an actual rate of growth, the values of $I + X$ and $S + M$ need not be equal in the "intended" or *ex ante* sense. If they are not, the level of national income changes. At an equilibrium level of national income, $I + X$ equals $S + M$ in both the intended and realized senses. But the equilibrium condition of national income is no guarantee of external equilibrium. There may be a passive balance on current account equal to the excess of home investment over home saving. This passive balance will be financed by a net capital inflow or gold outflow; in effect, the foreigner is providing the deficiency in home savings. Or there may be an active balance on current account equal to the excess of home saving over home investment; foreign investment is then covering the excess saving, and the active balance is being matched by a net flow of investment abroad or gold inflow.

This fundamental relationship can also be expressed diagrammatically, as in Fig. 6. The export function $X$, which includes all credit items on current account, is represented as autonomous with respect to the country's national income, since it is assumed that changes in the country's imports are too small to have a substantial influence upon the income of foreign countries to which the country exports. The other functions, however, are represented as dependent on the level of national income: imports $M$, which include all debits on current account, home investment $I$, and saving $S$ are all

---

[4] This does not allow for government expenditures and taxes, or else assumes that these are equal. More generally, the equation may be written $I + X + G = S + M + T$, where $G$ represents government expenditures and $T$ taxes.

shown to be greater the higher the level of national income.[5] Added horizontally, the functions give $I + X$ and $S + M$.

The intersection of $I + X$ with $S + M$ denotes the equilibrium level of income $OY_o$, to which actual income tends if a departure is made from $P$. But at any particular moment of

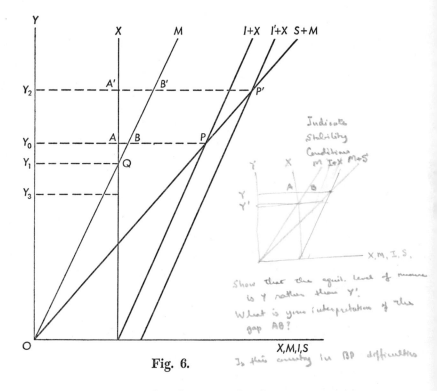

**Fig. 6.**

[5] For simplicity, we assume that the marginal and average propensities to consume are equal and remain constant through the time under consideration; similarly, for the marginal and average propensities to import. The savings schedule and the import schedule then begin at the origin, rather than at some point on the ordinate above the origin. The steepness of the investment function is due to the small amount of induced investment in a poor country.

time the actual income level need not be $OY_o$, for the relation $I + X = S + M$ is, of course, simply an accounting identity, with all the magnitudes interpreted as being "actual." Although the "actual" magnitudes must obey this identity, one or more of the "actual" magnitudes need not equal the "desired" magnitudes, and the economy can be out of equilibrium. Only if the "actual" savings, investment, and imports are also "desired" or "normal" magnitudes will the relation $I + X = S + M$ disclose the equilibrium level of income.

Even if this equilibrium condition of national income holds, however, it does not follow that the balance of payments will necessarily also be in equilibrium at that level of income. The balance of payments will be in equilibrium only if $X$ equals $M$, unless the deficit on current account is being offset by an equivalent amount of acceptable borrowing which gives a surplus on long-term capital account. But at the income level of $OY_o$, in Fig. 6, $M$ exceeds $X$ by the amount $AB$. Indeed, as long as the level of income is greater than $OY_1$, there will be a passive balance on current account which will require a gold outflow or a short-term capital inflow, if it is not counter-balanced by a long-term capital inflow.

3.    We may now explore the more common sources of external imbalance for a developing country. Assume that the country's level of income is initially $OY_1$ in Fig. 6 (the initial $I + X$ line would then be to the left of that drawn in Fig. 6). At this level of income, exports equal imports. If the country then embarks upon a development program which provides for an increase in the level of investment, $I + X$ will shift to the right by the amount of the increased investment, say to $I' + X$, and income will rise to $OY_2$. A passive balance on current account then arises in the amount $A'B'$. If the coun-

try had begun its development from a base income below
$OY_1$, say $OY_3$, income could have grown to $OY_1$ before the
original export surplus became converted to an import surplus. Sooner or later, however, the initial margin is dissipated, and the problem of disequilibrium emerges.

The problem might be eased by an expansion in exports.
But even in the favorable event that the development program supports an increased supply of exports (as experience
shows, it could just as likely hamper exports), the increase
in exports will tend to lag behind the rise in investment, and
the $I$ curve then shifts more rapidly to the right than does the
$X$ curve. The lead of $I$ over $X$ will be more pronounced under the following conditions: the larger is the proportion of
new investment that goes to non-export sectors of the economy; the more inelastic is the supply of exports; and the
more the home consumption of exportables increases as income rises.

Nor will the difficulty be easily removed even if after a
certain time lag the exports do increase more readily. For as
exports increase, the level of income will also rise, and so will
imports. It is therefore a problem of not only increasing exports by an amount sufficient to remove the initial gap $A'B'$,
which has resulted from the increase in investment, but also
by an additional amount which will offset the induced rise
in imports. The increase in imports may be expressed as
$\Delta M = m(\Delta Y)$, where $m$ is the marginal propensity to import.
We know that income will rise until the increase in $M + S$
equals the increase in $X + I$, or until $(m + s - i)\Delta Y = \Delta X$,
where $s$ and $i$ are the marginal propensities to save and invest, respectively. Thus,

$$\Delta Y = \frac{1}{m + s - i}(\Delta X),$$

and the induced imports are equal to

$$m(\Delta Y) = \frac{m}{m + s - i}\,(\Delta X).$$

To remove the deficit on current account which appears after investment increases, exports must therefore expand not only by the amount of the original gap $A'B'$, but by

$$A'B' + \frac{m}{m + s - i}\,(A'B').$$

The analysis has so far assumed constant propensities. But it is extreme—especially in the case of a developing country—to suppose that the import, saving, and investment coefficients remain constant over any long period. If we allow for changes in these coefficients, the balance of payments problem may become even more severe, unless there is a sufficient increase in the propensity to save, for the propensity to import is likely to rise, particularly during the early phases of the country's development. Although it will differ according to the character of the particular investment plan, the proportion of investment expenditure that must be directed to imports of capital goods is likely to be high. Since the import component of aggregate investment is much higher than the import component of consumption, there will be a rise in imports as the share of investment in the national product increases in relation to that of consumption.[6] Moreover, as personal incomes rise, the demand for imported consumer goods also tends to be high. Even if the additional investment is designed to produce substitutes for these imported consumer goods, there will still be a high income elasticity of demand for these imports during the gestation period of the

[6] Cf. Hal B. Lary, "Economic Development and the Capacity to Import—National Policies," *Lectures on Economic Development,* Faculty of Economics, Istanbul University, 1958, p. 133.

investment. Alternatively, if prior to the investment the government had already imposed controls on these imports in order to promote a home market for the larger output of import substitutes, the import content of the investment would then exceed the import coefficient of consumption *a fortiori*.

There is also a tendency for a developing country's marginal propensity to import to become greater as the level of income rises.[7] In part, this is because there is not a once-for-all introduction of the advanced countries' exports, but rather a more gradual process of preliminary "want development" for such commodities;[8] and these commodities, especially consumer goods, are of such a nature that they enter into the poor country's standard of consumption only after the country's income has risen above a certain minimum level. Over the long period the distribution of income in the poor country might also shift in favor of profits and rents, since, as the level of activity rises, numerous intermediary traders emerge and benefit from the secular inflationary pressures, the demand for land increases, and money wages do not rise commensurately because of the abundance of unskilled labor without bargaining power. Traders and landlords may be expected to have a higher marginal propensity to import than other classes, so that again the marginal propensity to import for the community will tend to increase as the level of income rises. With the shift of population away from a rural to an urban environment, the demand for imported goods will also increase as the pattern of consumer expenditures changes, and a higher proportion of income is used for the purchase of imported goods.

[7] The import function would then, of course, no longer be represented by a straight line in Fig. 6.

[8] Elizabeth E. Hoyt, "Want Development in Underdeveloped Areas," *Journal of Political Economy*, June, 1951, pp. 194-202.

Thus, there remains the basic problem that, in the course of development, the rate of growth of imports tends to be more rapid than the rate of growth of national output, and the demand for imports tends to exceed the export-based capacity to import—especially during the early phases when the increase in investment is sizeable and structural changes are considerable. The poor country then confronts a conflict between accelerating its internal development and maintaining external balance.

**4.** Another method for determining whether the pace of development has to be restrained for the sake of external balance, is to specify the critical level of investment above which external imbalance will result. This can be done in terms of the Harrod-Domar theory, as follows.[9]

Let $\sigma, \left(\dfrac{\Delta O_t}{\Delta K_{t-1}}\right)$, be the reciprocal of the marginal capital-output ratio, assumed constant. The expansion of productive capacity in period $t$ will then equal the investment of the previous period $t-1$ (the length of the gestation period of the investment), multiplied by $\sigma$, or $\Delta O_t = I_{t-1} \cdot \dfrac{\Delta O_t}{\Delta K_{t-1}}$.

Since the marginal propensity to consume domestic goods ($c$) is equal to $(1-s-m)$, the portion of the increased output that is available for an increase in domestic investment and for exports is

$$\Delta I_t + \Delta X_t = \Delta O_t - (1-s-m)\,\Delta O_t.$$

[9] Cf. J. C. Ingram, "Growth in Capacity and Canada's Balance of Payments," *American Economic Review*, March, 1957, pp. 95-97; K. K. Kurihara, "Economic Development and the Balance of Payments," *Metroeconomica*, March, 1958, pp. 16-27.

Or, $\Delta I_t + \Delta X_t = (s + m) I_{t-1} \cdot \sigma.$

While the rise in exports is $\Delta X_t = (s + m) I_{t-1} \cdot \sigma - \Delta I_t$, the increase in imports is $\Delta M_t = m \cdot I_{t-1} \cdot \sigma$, assuming that money income rises by the same proportion as output rises. If we now impose the condition that the economy expands without any deterioration in the balance on current account ($\Delta X = \Delta M$), it follows that

$\Delta X_t = (s + m) I_{t-1} \cdot \sigma - \Delta I_t = m \cdot I_{t-1} \cdot \sigma.$
Or,

$$\frac{\Delta I_t}{I_{t-1}} = s \cdot \sigma.$$

That is, the maximum rate of growth in investment that can be sustained without encountering balance of payments difficulties is equal to $s \cdot \sigma$. If investment grows at a higher rate, the growth in imports will outstrip the rise in exports, and the developing country will have to lose international reserves, or else receive an inflow of capital.

The ceiling on the rate of increase in investment would be higher, however, if we were to allow for the operation of other factors that may raise income, such as an increase in the labor force or improvements in land utilization as investment occurs. If $k$ represents the rate of increase in output due to these other factors, the maximum rate of growth of investment may be increased by the amount $k$, so that $\frac{\Delta I_t}{I_{t-1}} = s \cdot \sigma + k.$ An increase in $s$ would also reduce the balance of payments pressure. Similarly, if instead of assuming a constant $m$ we allowed for a shift in demand away from imports to domestic products as the result of investment in import-competing industries, the rate of increase in investment could be higher. Or if the investment raises productivity in the export industries, and rates of factor remuneration rise less rapidly, thereby allowing price reductions, and the price elasticity of demand for imports from the developing country is greater than unity, then the rate of increase in investment could again be higher.

Although allowance for these changes reduces the pressure on the balance of payments, nonetheless it would indeed be fortuitous if $\sigma$, $m$, $s$, and changes in productivity in the export sector should always change in such a way as to remove completely the balance of payments restraint. Changes in the parameters may allow the rate of increase in investment to rise for some time, but at some point the rate of increase will become too high to allow balance of payments equilibrium.

5.    In demonstrating that there will be no change in the balance on current account as long as any increase in desired investment is matched by a concurrent increase of desired saving, the preceding analysis reiterates the fundamental principle that external imbalance can be avoided if the investment is financed by non-inflationary methods. As long as investment expenditure is not increased by inflationary means, it will not cause any balance of payments deficit during the operation of the investment even though the investment itself may entail some increase in imports. For, regardless of its character, the output created by the investment allows aggregate supply to keep pace with aggregate demand, thereby removing pressure on the balance of payments. When the output is either export-creating or import-saving, it will directly improve the balance of payments. But the remaining alternative—an expansion in output for the domestic market—will also be import-saving, even though the substitution of domestic goods for imports is made only indirectly. Since the investment is non-inflationary, national expendi-

ture does not exceed national output; therefore, to buy the additional output from the new investment on the home market, there must be a reduction in imports. Such a switch of expenditure from imports will offset any increase in imports caused by the investment in the home industry.[10]

It must be emphasized that since inflation is an over-all problem in the economy, its adverse effects on the balance of payments do not depend on any particular distribution of investment. What matters for the avoidance of balance of payments problems is not the composition of the investment, but whether the investment is financed by non-inflationary means and whether it provides the highest possible social marginal product. It is erroneous to believe that balance of payments problems can only be avoided if the investment is directed toward export or import-competing industries. For, as long as investment is making the greatest possible contribution to an expansion in national output, and is not giving rise to inflation, it will also be aiding the balance of payments. To allocate investment arbitrarily to import-competing or export industries, instead of in accordance with the principle of acquiring the maximum marginal productivity from investment, is to be misled by a narrow "commodity approach" to balance of payments policy; it fails to recognize the over-all contribution of investment to national output and thereby indirectly to the balance of payments.[11]

When, however, national expenditure increases by infla-

[10] Cf. A. E. Kahn, "Investment Criteria in Development Programs," *Quarterly Journal of Economics,* February, 1951, pp. 42-47; Ragnar Nurkse, "International Trade Theory and Development Policy," H. S. Ellis, ed., *Economic Development for Latin America,* St. Martin's Press, 1961, pp. 259-260.

[11] Ragnar Nurkse, *Problems of Capital Formation in Underdeveloped Countries,* Basil Blackwell, 1953, pp. 137-138; "International Trade Theory and Development Policy," *op. cit.,* pp. 262-263.

tionary methods—through private or public deficit spending, or through dissaving—the expenditure will exceed the increase in output, and an external imbalance will result. For, in this case, to buy the new products on the home market, expenditure does not have to be diverted away from imports. An excess of spending over income at home will be taken out in an external deficit; the imbalance between imports and exports is simply the reflection of an imbalance between domestic investment and saving or between government expenditure and taxation.

6.   It now appears that if a poor country has an external deficit caused by inflationary pressures, and it cannot borrow more abroad, its national expenditure must then be reduced to the level of its national output. Until there is internal stabilization the external disequilibrium will persist, since the total absorption of goods and services by households, firms, and government will continue to exceed the country's aggregate production plus any autonomous capital inflow. In this inflationary situation neither import restrictions nor devaluation alone will prove effective in removing the external imbalance; these measures must be supplemented by policies that will also lower the rate of absorption.

Only under highly restrictive conditions would import regulations or devaluation automatically have effects of the right character on absorption. Import regulations will not create their own "disabsorption" if the income formerly spent on imports is now simply diverted to domestic consumption. Barring a reduction in investment, if the income previously spent on imports does not now remain unspent, then domestic consumption increases, prices rise, and the volume of exports falls. Under these conditions, the strain on the balance of payments would be lessened only if there were an inelastic demand for exports, so that export revenue increased as export prices rose, and this increase in export revenue were saved. It is more likely, in the generality of cases, that the balance of payments repercussions of inflationary pressures will take the form of a weakening of the competitive position of exports, an increase in imports, a deterrence to the inflow of foreign capital, and an encouragement to capital flight.

Moreover, since import controls in themselves will not help to remove the cause of the disequilibrium, they can only continue to suppress the disequilibrium if they are retained on a long-run basis. The disadvantages of maintaining import regulations over long periods are, however, especially severe in a developing economy, for the continual reliance on import restrictions to protect international reserves will react adversely on production.[12] Bottlenecks in production will tend to occur when stocks of imported materials have been worked down to low levels. Behind the protection of the import regulations, monopoly elements may be strengthened, and distortions in production may give rise to unusual opportunities for private profits. The protection given by import control will tend not only to increase costs and thereby weaken the competitive position of the export industries, but also to divert resources to import-competing industries at the expense of export development. All these adverse effects attest to the basic difficulty that, when import controls are added on to an inflationary economy, the allocation of resources becomes even more distorted; in the absence of external competition, every new project appears profitable, but the result is low productivity as the economy strains in too many directions.

Under inflationary conditions, the other possibility—an ad-

[12] For an elaboration of the following points, see Eric Lundberg, "International Stability and the National Economy," Douglas Hague, ed., *Stability and Progress in the World Economy*, St. Martin's Press, 1958, pp. 216-218.

justment of the country's exchange rate—is also likely to prove ineffective. Even if the elasticity of demand for imports and the elasticity of supply for exports are sufficiently high to rule out the perverse case of devaluation, it is necessary, under conditions of full employment, that the devaluation be accompanied by a fall in aggregate real expenditure so as to allow an improvement in the trade balance through an increase in export volume and a fall in the import volume. When devaluation changes relative prices, resulting in an increase in the local currency prices of exports and imports relative to home prices, there must be a shift in demand away from export and import goods to domestic goods and a shift in home production in favor of exportables and import substitutes. These shifts have inflationary effects which will cancel the devaluation, unless they are counteracted by deflationary measures. If when a country devalues it does not also adopt measures to hold aggregate domestic expenditure constant, any increase in exports or decrease in imports resulting from devaluation will simply lead to an inflation of expenditure and renewed pressures on the balance of payments. It is therefore essential that monetary expansion not be allowed to offset the equilibrating effects of devaluation.

In the interests of stressing the view that domestic expenditure is a basic and deliberate policy variable for the maintenance of external balance, we have focused on an aggregate spending approach to balance of payments adjustment. But this approach should not be overemphasized to the neglect of the complementary role played by changes in relative prices (the elasticities approach). It should be recognized that if the money supply is kept constant, real absorption will be automatically reduced by the rise in the price level and the reduction in the real value of total cash balances as a result of the devaluation. Besides the effects on absorption of the rise in the level of prices, the relative price changes associated with a change in the terms of trade will also affect absorption, through both the income effects and substitution effects of the change in the terms of trade. In general, relative price changes and income-expenditure adjustments combine to determine the effects of a devaluation.[13]

When a policy of import control or devaluation is supplemented by adequate monetary and fiscal policies of "disabsorption," it may then be possible to remove the external balance without sacrificing internal balance. Such a combined policy of deflation accompanied by either import restriction or devaluation will allow a given improvement in the balance of payments to be attained at a higher level of employment than if deflation is used alone.[14] But since it will conflict with the development program if the required "disabsorption" of resources is sought through a restriction of investment and government expenditures, the brunt of the "disabsorption"

[13] For a well-balanced exposition, see S. C. Tsiang, "The Role of Money in Trade-Balance Stability: Synthesis of the Elasticity and Absorption Approaches," *American Economic Review*, December, 1961, pp. 912-936. Also, cf. S. S. Alexander, "Effects of a Devaluation: A Simplified Synthesis of Elasticities and Absorption Approaches," *American Economic Review*, March, 1959, pp. 22-42; Harry G. Johnson, *International Trade and Economic Growth*, George Allen & Unwin Ltd., 1958, chap. VI; F. Machlup, "Relative Prices and Aggregate Spending in the Analysis of Devaluation," *American Economic Review*, June, 1955, pp. 255-278.

[14] For an illuminating, albeit highly formal, analysis of the optimum combination of import restrictions, devaluation, and deflation, see M. F. W. Hemming and W. M. Corden, "Import Restriction as an Instrument of Balance of Payments Policy," *Economic Journal*, September, 1958, pp. 483-510.

For a comparison of the use of direct controls and of price adjustments in the light of their effects on the balance of payments and the level of real income in the different coutries, see J. E. Meade, *Balance of Payments*, Oxford University Press, 1951, chaps. XXI, XXIII, XXIV.

must fall on consumption. It is, however, difficult to mobilize additional saving out of current consumption. Reliance must then be placed on additional saving out of current increases in output. Although there is unlikely to be a voluntary increase in saving, even out of additions to income, the saving might be forced through taxation. If the import content of investment is higher than the import content of marginal consumption expenditures, the balance of payments situation will not be improved immediately, but it will be eased eventually as the investment results in additional domestic production and as resources are released from the domestic consumption sector for the export and import-competing sectors.

If efforts to increase domestic saving fail, the overabsorption must be covered by foreign borrowing of an autonomous or acceptable character. As long as a development program emphasizes investment, and there is a deficiency of home savings, an increased supply of long-term capital from foreign countries is needed. Historically, the investment expenditure which touched off the development process in many poor countries was financed by an inflow of foreign capital acceptable to both lender and borrower. This capital inflow, in turn, reduced the need for internal and external controls or continual depreciation. Nonetheless, this did not mean that adjustments within the balance of payments were unnecessary. Indeed, the foreign borrowings presented substantial problems: initially, the accomplishment of the real transfer of the capital and the confinement of the current account deficit to the capital account surplus, and subsequently, the servicing of the debt. These problems will be examined in Chapter 5.

# 5 *Foreign Capital*

1. The traditional theory of international capital movements has been concerned mainly with the mechanism of adjustment in the balance of payments. In the context of development, this theory should be re-examined to determine not only how the long-run forces of development may affect the transfer mechanism, but also to consider the impact of international investment on the development process itself.

Although it is common in the extensive literature on development to acknowledge the importance of foreign capital, the discussion is usually at too remote a level of generality and is insufficiently related to fundamental problems of development. There is still, as Nurkse emphasized, a need for "a theory of capital movements that is concerned with capital as a factor of production" and a theory that "would direct attention to the unequal proportions in which capital cooperates with labor and land in the different parts of the world; to the technical forms which capital should assume in response to different relative factor endowments; to the relations between capital movements, population growth and migration; and to other such fundamental matters. Only fragments of this type of capital-movement theory exist today, but the great awakening is forcing the attention of economists all over the world to these basic questions—with some benefit, one may hope, not only to the theory of capital formation and development, but to international economics generally."[1]

Responding to some of these questions, this chapter analyzes the more important developmental aspects of the international movement of capital.

**2.**    Any discussion of this topic must acknowledge that the role of external capital is now intimately linked to development planning. Even though the argument for capital accumulation as the central objective of a development program is often set forth too naively in terms of macro-economic theories that rely on capital-output ratios, the theoretical analysis of development still gives particular emphasis to an increase in the capital supply. The historical interpretation of development also underlines the contribution of capital accumulation to a more rapid rate of development. It is not surprising that, on the side of policy, development plans should also reflect this emphasis.

Most poor countries now view their need for foreign capital and how it is to be utilized from the standpoint of their development programs. Capital-exporting countries have even encouraged the practice of development planning as a prerequisite for the receipt of public foreign investment. Through a variety of policy measures, the recipient countries also in-

[1] Ragnar Nurkse, *Problems of Capital Formation in Underdeveloped Countries,* Basil Blackwell, 1953, p. 131.

fluence the magnitude, composition, and use of their foreign borrowings. Thus, unlike the classical theory of international capital movements, or historical interpretations of earlier periods of foreign investment, the present role of foreign capital in poor countries cannot be considered apart from development planning.

3.   The foreign capital requirements of a development plan can be identified with the need for additional real resources in order to achieve the plan's objectives. If the development program entails greater investment than can be sustained by the level of domestic savings, and it is desired to undertake the additional expenditure without generating inflation, then the excess of domestic expenditure over current output must be covered by external financing. Although it is not possible to identify any one source of funds with a specific type of use, it is basic to an understanding of the developmental role of capital imports to recognize that net capital imports can offset or "finance" all three of the following differences as aggregates: (1) value of products used *minus* value of products produced domestically; (2) net investment minus net domestic savings; (3) value of imported goods and services, including factor payments *minus* value of exported goods and services, including factor receipts.[2] When the claims of the development plan exceed the available domestic resources, the shortfall in real resources must be removed by using foreign resources. The gap in real resources is thus reflected in a foreign exchange gap; an inflow of foreign capital (or fall in foreign exchange reserves) will be necessary

[2] Simon Kuznets, "International Differences in Capital Formation and Financing," National Bureau of Economic Research, *Capital Formation and Economic Growth,* Princeton University Press, 1955, pp. 34-35.

to give command over the additional resources.

Since they depend on projections of foreign exchange earnings and foreign exchange expenditures during the plan period, estimates of the foreign capital requirements are necessarily inexact. The total foreign exchange resources available for imports are estimated from projections of the sum of export earnings, net invisible receipts (excluding official donations), and net capital transactions (excluding fresh receipts of official loans and private foreign investment). From this total, a deduction may be made for essential imports that might be termed "maintenance imports"—that is, inescapable imports such as raw materials, intermediate products, foodstuffs, and capital goods for replacement.[3] The balance then constitutes the foreign exchange resources available for "development imports"—that is, for the direct import requirements of the plan's investment targets in the public and private sectors. To the extent that foreign exchange requirements for "development imports" exceed the availability of foreign exchange, the plan will have to be financed by foreign savings in the form of a capital inflow (neglecting any possible use of existing foreign exchange reserves).

When estimates of the need for foreign capital are made at the beginning of the plan period, they are likely to turn out to be quite wide of the mark during the course of the plan period, and the plan must then be revised. Most programs have been in error in underestimating foreign capital re-

[3] This procedure is adopted in Indian planned development; Government of India, Planning Commission, *Indian Third Five Year Plan: A Draft Outline,* June, 1960, p. 53.

For a generalized theoretical analysis of the calculation of foreign exchange requirements of investment programs, see A. K. Sen, "A Note on the Foreign Exchange Requirement of Development Plans," *Economia Internazionale,* March, 1957, pp. 248-257.

quirements. In some cases this has been due to over-optimistic projections of export earnings; more frequently, it has resulted from underestimating import requirements for both "maintenance imports" and "development imports." This is understandable, since it is extremely difficult to predict the import content of new projects and also the import-saving that may result from the whole development of domestic output.

Regardless of errors in estimating the extent to which fulfillment of the plan must rely on foreign capital, the fundamental principle remains: the dependence on external capital limits the size of the plan. Since most development plans are predicated on the achievement of an investment target to bring about the rate of income growth postulated by the plan, the question of capital provision is of prime importance. In a closed economy this would by necessity be simply a matter of sufficient domestic saving. In poor countries, however, domestic resources are generally too limited for the home manufacture of capital equipment; consequently, when given the opportunity of foreign trade, a large proportion of the required capital equipment will be imported. Even if all investment projects were labor-intensive, but the country had to import foodstuffs, the amount of additional labor that could be employed would then be effectively limited by the amount of foreign exchange available to buy food (the real wages of the workers). An increase in domestic savings can help to finance these essential imports (whether for plant, equipment, or food) only to the extent that it reduces imports of consumption goods, or releases resources for an expansion in exports. A lowering of home consumption, however, will not have significant effects in reducing consumption imports if these imports constitute only a small proportion of total imports, or if consumption goods are in very inelastic demand. Nor will it help to expand exports if the barrier to additional exports is to be found on the side of demand rather than on the side of supply. The question of capital provision is therefore not merely a matter of saving: it is a balance of payments question.[4] Since the investment program results in rapidly rising imports, the plan has to be financed by an inflow of capital to the extent that foreign exchange receipts on current account fall short of foreign exchange requirements, unless the country is able and willing to fill the gap with international reserves.

While the dependence on external financing may have to be large during the early years of the development program, most plans aim for a progressive reduction in foreign aid and an eventual approach to a self-financing plan. To achieve this, the plan relies on a high marginal rate of savings; it is expected that the proportion that can be saved out of an increase in output will be much higher than average savings at the start of the plan period. The proportion of national income invested and financed by domestic savings would then increase, and the ratio of net foreign capital imports to additional investment would fall. Since profits provide a major source of savings, there are grounds for expecting an increase in home savings relative to income when an expansion of the capitalist sector is facilitated and government enterprises begin to yield operating surpluses.[5] A higher savings rate may

[4] An illuminating discussion of the practical consequences to be drawn from this argument is given by J. R. Hicks, *Essays in World Economics*, Oxford University Press, 1959, pp. 204-207; I. M. D. Little, "The Third Five Year Plan and the Strategy of Indian Development," *The Economic Weekly*, June, 1960, pp. 887-888.

[5] Cf. W. A. Lewis, *The Theory of Economic Growth*, George Allen & Unwin Ltd., 1955, pp. 236-239. The expected increase in profits applies not only to private capitalists; as Lewis states, it is just as relevant to State capitalism, or to any form of economic organization where capital

also result if the composition of output changes in favor of more industrial activities with high marginal rates of saving. It will still be difficult, however, to realize a substantially higher marginal savings rate without forcing public saving through additional taxation and increasing tax revenues as a proportion of national income.

From the standpoint of the balance of payments, the reliance on foreign capital will also diminish if, as development proceeds, the composition of investment alters towards projects with a lower import content. Furthermore, an economizing on other imports will result directly from control of inessential imports and from measures designed to reallocate resources towards the production of home substitutes for imports. Provided there is no inflationary financing, import-saving will also be indirectly fostered by the growth in total domestic output and a diversion of purchasing power to the products of the expanding industries. In countries that import foodstuffs, the success of agricultural development in expanding the home production of foodstuffs will be especially instrumental in replacing imports. Finally, export promotion policies may increase export revenue, not merely from efforts to raise productivity in traditional export activities, but even more so by adding to the value of exports by selling them at a more highly processed stage and by extending the range of export items.

**4.** In formulating a development plan, it is deceptively simple to consider foreign capital merely as the residual means of financing the plan. The full implications of external financing can not be appreciated by a simple arithmetic

---

is used to employ people, and where, after payment of wages and salaries, a substantial surplus remains of which a large part is reinvested productively.

exercise of starting from a calculation of the amount of investment needed to achieve a desired growth rate, estimating home savings, and then desiring foreign capital to cover the balance. A less mechanical, more comprehensive analysis of the role of foreign capital is needed. In the broadest sense, the analysis should consider how the capital inflow relates to a greater national effort to increase the rate of development. More specifically, it should examine the differential impact of various forms of foreign capital receipts, their costs and benefits, and the transfer problem.

At the outset of a development plan, the demand for foreign capital should be restrained to a level that is economically warranted. The demand ought to be tempered by the requirement that the external capital should add to—not substitute for—the country's own developmental efforts. Foreign capital gives an additional command over resources, but if it is to result in a higher rate of investment, it must be prevented from simply substituting for domestic sources of financing investment, and it should not be dissipated in supporting higher personal consumption or an increase in non-development current expenditure by the government.

If current consumption were to be bolstered through external financing, the scope for the use of foreign capital could be practically without bounds. When we exclude this use, the economically warranted demand for foreign capital is limited by the recipient country's absorptive capacity—that is, by its ability to use capital productively. At least in the short run, even if not in the longer run, there may be a limit to how much foreign investment can be effectively used when the investment must not only cover its costs but also yield a reasonable increase in income. At the beginning of the plan, the country's technical absorptive capacity will be determined by the extent to which certain conditions neces-

sary for the productive utilization of capital are already existent in the economy. In general, the capacity to absorb
external resources for productive investment purposes will
be low when there are inadequate public overhead facilities,[6]
administrative and organizational bottlenecks, deficient qual-
ities of entrepreneurship, shortages of complementary natural
resources, scarcities of trained manpower, low geographic
and occupational mobility of labor, and narrow localized
markets.[7] These handicaps may prevent some of the projects
in the development plan from ever being implemented in the
first instance. In other cases, the project may be completed
but not utilized fully or efficiently. And in still other situations, the limited supply of complementary factors and
facilities may result in a sharp decline in the marginal productivity of capital as capital accumulates. The marginal productivity of capital in a poor country may be high at the
outset of an investment program, but if diminishing returns
to capital are to be forestalled, it is necessary to eliminate
the bottlenecks, increase the supply of factors cooperating
with capital, and achieve more rapid technological progress.

Once the pace of development gains momentum, the absorptive capacity will be higher. With greater productivity
and a better mechanism for resource allocation, the rate of
effective utilization of foreign capital would continually increase. At the same time, however, the need for external cap-

---

[6] The very object of public foreign investment may, of course, be the
creation of these facilities. In the absence of public overheads, however, the capacity to absorb private direct investment will be limited.

[7] Noneconomic aspects of the social systems in the poor countries are
also important in accounting for the low capacity to absorb capital productively. See, for instance, Marion J. Levy, Jr., "Some 'Social Obstacles' to 'Capital Formation' in 'Underdeveloped Areas'," National
Bureau of Economic Research, *Capital Formation and Economic
Growth, op. cit.,* pp. 450-497.

ital tends to be less pressing, as saving can now be more readily extracted from other sources, and a given amount of capital can be used more productively.

**5.** Going beyond these general comments on capital requirements and absorptive capacity, we may now analyze more directly the contribution that foreign investment can make to a country's development. This requires us to weigh the benefits of foreign investment against its costs in order to assess the difference made to the real income of the recipient country by the presence of foreign-owned capital.[8] For simplicity, we shall concentrate on private foreign investment, although the analysis, with modifications, may also be relevant for public borrowing.

There is a national economic gain from more capital imports if the value added to output by the foreign capital is greater than the amount appropriated by the investor: social returns then exceed private returns.[9] When foreign investment raises productivity, and this increase is not wholly appropriated by the investor, there must be a net addition to some other incomes. The direct benefits of foreign investment can then accrue to local factors of production in the form of higher real incomes, to consumers by way of lower prices, and to the government through higher tax revenue. In addition, there are likely to be indirect, but highly substantial, gains through the realization of external economies.

[8] Much of the following analysis has been suggested by Sir Donald MacDougall, "The Benefits and Costs of Private Investment from Abroad: A Theoretical Approach," *Economic Record*, March, 1960, pp. 13-35.

[9] We cannot, of course, identify the national economic interest in capital imports with the more general national interest that would have to include an assessment of political and social benefits and costs. In the present analysis, we set aside the noneconomic benefits and costs.

An inflow of foreign capital may be a major influence in raising labor's marginal productivity and increasing total real wages. Assuming two factors of production—capital and labor—the line $EG$ in Fig. 7 relates the marginal physical product of capital to the physical capital stock, given the amount of labor. If initially the capital stock is $AB$, total output is

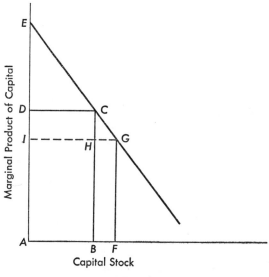

Fig. 7.

$ECBA$. Assuming that profits per unit of capital equal the marginal product of capital, and that the total capital stock $AB$ is domestically owned, total profits on domestic capital are $ABCD$, and total real wages are $CDE$.

If there is now an inflow of foreign capital in the amount $BF$, total output increases by the amount $BFGC$. The foreign capital now earns $BFGH$ of this amount. Since the marginal product of capital, and hence the profit rate, have fallen, total profits on domestic capital are reduced to *ABHI*, but the total real wages of labor are now *GIE*. Although the increase in real wages amounts to *DCGI*, most of labor's gain—the amount *DCHI*—is merely a redistribution from domestic capitalists. Given the marginal product curve, both the redistribution effect and the net gain to domestic factors, represented by the triangle *CGH*, will be larger, the larger is the inflow of foreign capital.

The presence of foreign capital may not only raise the productivity of a given amount of labor; it may also allow a larger labor force to be employed. This may be most relevant for heavily-populated poor countries where the population pressures are taken out through unemployment or underemployment in the rural sector. If, as is frequently contended, a shortage of capital limits the employment of labor from the rural sector in the industrial sector where wages are higher, an inflow of foreign capital would make possible more employment in the advanced sector. The international movement of capital thus serves as an alternative to the migration of labor from the poor country; when outlets for the emigration of "surplus" labor are restricted, the substitution of domestic migration of labor into the advanced sector becomes the most feasible solution. The social benefit from the foreign investment in the advanced sector would then be greater than the profits on this investment, for the wages received by the newly employed exceed their marginal productivity in the rural sector, and this excess should be added as a national gain.[10]

Some of the benefits of foreign investment may also accrue to consumers. This is especially likely for direct foreign in-

[10] Cf. MacDougall, *op. cit.*, pp. 21, 35; T. Balogh and P. P. Streeten, "Domestic versus Foreign Investment," *Bulletin of the Oxford University Institute of Statistics*, August, 1960, p. 220.

vestment. When the investment is cost-reducing in a particular industry, there may be a gain not only to the suppliers
of factors in this industry through higher factor prices but
also to consumers of the product through lower product
prices. If the investment is product-improving or product-
innovating, consumers may then benefit from better quality
products or new products.

In order to have local factors of production and consumers
enjoy part of the benefit of higher productivity in enterprises
established by foreign capital, the overseas withdrawal by
foreign investors must be less than the increase in output.
However, even if the entire increase in productivity accrues
as foreign profits, this requirement may still be met to the
extent that the government taxes foreign profits.

**6.** From the standpoint of contributing to the development
process, the most substantial benefit of foreign investment
will probably arise from external economies. Direct investment brings to the recipient country not only capital but also
technical personnel, technological knowledge, and innovations in products and production techniques. By the example
they set, foreign firms may then promote the diffusion of
technological advance to the rest of the economy. This benefit may be significant insofar as through imitation domestic
firms might make up for their own lack of innovations. In
addition, foreign investment may result in the training of
labor in new skills, and the knowledge gained by these workers may spread to other parts of the labor force, or this labor
may be later employed by local firms.

When foreign capital is used to develop the borrowing
country's infrastructure and social capital it can also be a
strong stimulus to additional domestic investment. Even if
the foreign investment is in one industry, it may still encour-

age more domestic investment by reducing costs or creating demand in other industries. Profits may then rise and lead to expansion in these other industries. In the case of a poor country, in which there are so many specific scarcities, the breaking of a bottleneck is a common form of cost-reducing investment. This raises profits on all underutilized productive capacity and in all those lines where the exploitation of economies of scale had previously been restricted.[11]

It is also possible that foreign investment in one industry will make the product of this industry cheaper, so that another industry that uses this product will then enjoy an external pecuniary economy. This, in turn, means more profits and an expansion in the second industry. The investment in the first industry may also give rise to profits in industries that supply inputs to the first industry, in industries that produce complementary products, and in industries that produce goods bought by the factor-owners who now have higher real incomes. The initial foreign investment may thus produce external investment incentives through demand creation in other industries, thereby setting up a whole series of domestic investments.

7.   Although the foregoing effects of foreign investment are beneficial, they must be qualified by possible costs to the borrowing country. Against these gains must be set the possibilities of adverse effects on domestic saving, deterioration in the terms of trade, and problems of balance of payments adjustment.[12]

Insofar as foreign investment results in a higher income

[11] Cf. MacDougall, *op. cit.*, p. 23; Balogh and Streeten, *op. cit.*, p. 217.
[12] While the discussion here is theoretical, Chapter 7 considers the broader contention that foreign investment has historically limited the development of the borrowing country; see pp. 166–173.

in the recipient country, it should also lead to a higher level of domestic savings. This effect may be thwarted, however, by a redistribution of income away from capital if the foreign investment reduces profits on domestic capital. Although this indirect cost of foreign investment should be recognized, it is unlikely to be of much consequence in practice. It is more probable that foreign capital, whether in the form of public investment or private direct investment, will be complementary with domestic investment and will give rise to higher incomes and profits in other sectors. Foreign investment may have its greatest effect in stimulating domestic capital formation through the side of demand, but it can also contribute to it from the side of saving. Domestic measures are, however, necessary to realize an increase in the country's marginal rate of savings. Since an increase in the marginal savings rate is of predominant importance for achieving a self-sustaining process of development, it is essential that the full potential from foreign investment be realized through domestic measures that mobilize as savings a large part of the income generated by foreign investment. It is also necessary to provide for the interdependence of internal and external sources of finance. Domestic measures that promote internal financial institutions to mobilize domestic savings may open up a wider variety of sources and forms of capital inflow, allow supplementary domestic saving to be combined with foreign capital for expenditure on local resources, and facilitate the exploitation of new opportunities and growth of subsidiary activities in response to foreign-financed sectors.[13]

**8.** The possible effects of foreign investment on the terms of trade are usually related to the transfer problem—the

[13] Cf. Nural Islam, *Foreign Capital and Economic Development: Japan, India, and Canada,* Charles E. Tuttle Co., 1960, p. 242.

terms of trade normally tend to improve with an inflow of capital, then tend to worsen when there is subsequently a return flow of capital from the borrowing country. We shall consider these effects in the next section as part of the broader problem of balance of payments adjustment.

Aside from these transfer effects, foreign investment may also affect the terms of trade through structural changes associated with the pattern of development that results from the capital inflow. If foreign investment leads to an increase in the borrowing country's rate of development without any change in the terms of trade, then the country's growth of real income will be the same as its growth of output. Only under exceptional conditions, however, is this likely. Instead, it is to be expected that the terms of trade will alter—improving or worsening, depending on various possible changes at home and abroad in the supply and demand for exports, import-substitutes, and domestic commodities. We have already considered in Chapters 2 and 3 under what conditions the commodity terms of trade will turn against a country when it accumulates capital. The same analysis can be applied to an inflow of foreign capital when it results in a higher rate of capital formation.

If the pattern of development associated with foreign investment involves a deterioration in the borrowing country's commodity terms of trade, then the net gain from foreign capital will be diminished. It is improbable, however, that foreign investment would cause any substantial deterioration. For if an unfavorable shift resulted from an export bias on the side of consumption, it would probably be controlled through import restrictions. And if it resulted from an export bias in production, it would be most likely due to private direct investment in the export sector, but this inflow of foreign capital would diminish as export prices fell, thereby limiting the deterioration in the terms of trade. Moreover, if the deterioration comes through an export bias in production, it is possible that the factoral and the income terms of trade might still improve even though the commodity terms worsen.

9.   More important than the foregoing, are the possible adverse effects of international capital movements upon the balance of payments. Although access to foreign capital will ease the undertaking of a development program, it may give rise to problems of balance of payments adjustment. The debtor country will confront transfer problems—initially, with the accomplishment of the real transfer of the capital, then with the need to confine the current account deficit to the capital account surplus, and subsequently with the servicing of the debt.

If the transfer mechanism does not operate rapidly and smoothly, a disequilibrium will persist in the balance of payments of the lending and borrowing countries. We have seen that a developing economy is especially susceptible to a large potential deficit on current account. The problem of effecting the real transfer may therefore be not so much that of acquiring an import surplus on current account equal to the surplus on long term capital account as that of preventing a potential deficit on current account from becoming actually realized—in other words, restraining the demand for foreign exchange within limits given by the supply of foreign exchange. Subsequently, the amount of foreign exchange required to service the foreign debts might become larger than the amount of foreign exchange being supplied by new foreign borrowings; the transfer mechanism will then have to create a surplus on current account equal to the debit item on account of the payment of interest, dividends, profits and amortization on the foreign borrowings.

For the young debtors, it is significant that the very forces of development may themselves facilitate balance of payments equilibrium. Since the foreign borrowings are for developmental purposes, imports from the lending country frequently follow directly on the borrowings. To the extent that the loans are directly expended in the lending country, there is no transfer problem. If, however, the foreign investment is autonomous rather than a tied loan,[14] only a portion of the investment is likely to induce imports directly from the lending country. There is still a problem for the creditor country of successfully transferring the foreign capital in the form of an export surplus.

When attention is given to the forces of development, a full explanation of the transfer mechanism extends beyond the classical analysis of sectional price changes among domestic, export, and import-competing commodities. Especially relevant for poor countries, is the fact that the capital borrowings stimulate employment and output and thereby induce imports through the increase in real income. If the borrowing leads to monetary expansion, the ensuing inflation will also stimulate imports.

Let us investigate the consequences of a capital export from a lending country $L$ to a borrowing country $B$ as a result of long-term portfolio investment and direct investment in $B$ by residents of $L$. We are concerned with the real transfer. The tendency for $B$ to acquire an import surplus will be stronger under the following conditions: the greater is the

[14] Although it is commonly believed that a tied loan automatically generates additional exports from the lending country, this may simply be illusory when the "tied" exports would have taken place anyhow, or when they merely replace other "untied" exports. These possible cases are discussed by James E. Meade, *Trade and Welfare*, Oxford University Press, 1955, pp. 474-475.

inflation of domestic expenditure in $B$; the more $B$'s prices rise relatively to $L$'s; and the higher are the price elasticities of demand for imports in $L$ and $B$. Our problem, therefore, is to determine how the development process affects domestic expenditure, prices, and the price elasticity of demand for imports.

Consider the situation in which new investment opportunities occur in $B$, or an expansion develops in an existing industry in $B$, perhaps in the export sector in response to rising world prices for export products. Part of the new investment might be financed from domestic savings, but part might also come from borrowings in $L$. In $B$, the demand for capital borrowings from $L$ should be greater, in the schedule sense, under the following conditions: the smaller is the supply of $B$'s domestic savings; the more domestic activity expands in $B$; and the more the cost of borrowing rises in $B$ relatively to the cost in $L$.

With the aid of funds from abroad, not only can an expansion in $B$ be initiated, but it can also be prolonged for a longer period than would be possible with only domestically-financed investment. Of special interest is the possibility that the expansion process in $B$ might in itself cause $B$ to have a passive balance on current account that offsets the active balance on capital account. As $B$ undergoes a more rapid rate of development, the re-equilibrating mechanism may operate quickly and smoothly on the balance of payments for several reasons.

First, the multiplier effects of the initial volume of investment raises the level of income in $B$. By increasing domestic expenditure and raising income, the investment stimulates imports into $B$ from $L$. The increase in imports need not, of course, consist of capital goods. Capital can be transferred through an increase in imports of consumption goods into $B$:

savings in $L$ can be lent to investors in $B$ to spend on capital formation projects in $B$, and resources in $B$, which were previously used to produce consumption goods, can be released through the higher imports of such goods and used instead for capital development in $B$.

Further, the expansion in $B$ may involve changes in sectional prices that do not counteract the income effects but instead reinforce them. To have price variations stimulate an import surplus in $B$, the prices of import-competing goods in $B$ must rise relatively to the prices of $L$'s exports, while the prices of $B$'s exports rise more than the prices of $L$'s import-competing products. There must also be some elasticity of substitution between domestic and foreign commodities so that the price elasticity of demand for imports is sufficiently high.

A rise in domestic income, however, does not necessarily involve a parallel rise in the domestic price level, let alone sectional price changes of the right kind in terms of the adjustment mechanism. Whether it does so is a question of not only the influence of investment on money income, but also the influence of the investment on the current supply of goods. For, while the income effects depend primarily on the volume of investment, the price effects are determined to a considerable extent by the character of that investment.

If the marginal cost curves of import, export, and domestic commodities are horizontal over the relevant ranges of output and do not shift upwards, then price changes will not occur when demand increases in the schedule sense. The other extreme of perfectly inelastic supply curves would, of course, result in only increased prices. It is then, essentially, a matter of placing export, import, and domestic goods between these extremes and examining the relevant cost-price structures.

When new investment occurs in $B$, the expanding sectors of the economy draw resources away from other sectors. After a time, the level of money wages is especially likely to rise. If unit labor costs in the export and import-competing industries increase, there will then also be a tendency for the prices in these industries to rise. There will be even greater upward pressure on prices if, as demand shifts to these industries, a long period of gestation prevents additional supplies from becoming readily available on the market, or if production beyond the optimum capacity of plant and equipment creates bottlenecks.

Moreover, from the viewpoint of $L$, the foreign investment may be at the expense of home investment, or $L$ may be experiencing a cyclical downswing. Therefore, when $B$'s demand for $L$'s exports increases, unemployed resources can be attracted to the export sector without a rise in wages or prices. Under these conditions, the commodity terms of trade deteriorate for $L$. Then, if the price elasticities of demand for imports are sufficiently high in $L$ and $B$, as they are likely to be the longer the period considered, the classical emphasis on price effects becomes relevant.

The above analysis suggests that, when proper account is taken of the development process which occurs in the borrowing country, the mechanism of adjustment might be explained more fully—especially for the case of private foreign investment—than it has been in traditional theory.[15]

**10.**   Although the expansionary forces in the recipient country facilitate the initial transfer of capital, they may at the

[15] For an application of this type of analysis, see the author's "Economic Development and the Transfer Mechanism: Canada, 1895-1913," *Canadian Journal of Economics and Political Science*, February, 1953, pp. 1-19.

same time create so high a demand for imports that the country has to avoid a "transfer problem in reverse."[16] For a poor country, the more crucial question posed by foreign investment is likely to be how to limit the import surplus to the total amount of foreign capital available, rather than how to create an import surplus in order to achieve the transfer in the first instance.

This type of "negative" transfer problem emerges when the complementary demands of the borrowing country are so strong that they give rise to an increased demand for foreign exchange that exceeds the increase in foreign exchange available from the capital inflow. This problem can be expressed more precisely in terms of an "expansion ratio," defined as the actual ratio of the rate of investment in the borrowing country over the initial rate of capital inflow.[17] Given the rate of capital inflow, marginal propensity to consume, and marginal propensity to import, there will be a certain maximum expansion ratio which designates the limit to which domestic investment, financed by foreign loans and by domestic credit expansion, can be increased without endangering the balance of payments.[18]

[16] C. P. Kindleberger, *International Economics*, Richard D. Irwin, Inc., 1953, p. 354.

[17] J. J. Polak, "Balance of Payments Problems of Countries Reconstructing with the Help of Foreign Loans," *Quarterly Journal of Economics*, February, 1943, p. 214.

[18] If the marginal propensity to save is 1/4, and the marginal propensity to import is 1/4, the maximum expansion ratio would be 2—that is, a level of investment of two times the level of capital inflow could be maintained without encountering an import surplus greater than the capital inflow. In this simple model, the multiplier ($k$) is 2, and the import demand ($\Delta M$) is 1/2 of the amount of investment ($\Delta I$), $[\Delta M = m(k\Delta I)]$, so that one dollar of domestic investment for each dollar of foreign-financed investment would use up the foreign investment in induced imports. If, in addition to the indirect demand

The tendency to exceed this maximum expansion ratio is especially strong for a poor country. This is because foreign investment not only entails its own demand for imports, but is also likely to raise the level of domestic spending and add to inflationary pressures, thereby inducing additional imports. As we have already noted, a capital inflow may stimulate domestic investment through demand creation in other industries and by producing investment incentives elsewhere in the economy. If there is an increase in investment beyond the foreign investment, and this is financed by credit creation, then the inflationary financing of investment will add to the demand for imports and may cause an increase in imports in excess of the supply of foreign exchange.

When foreign investment leads to a negative transfer problem, the debtor country has to endure a loss of international reserves, or else bear the costs of policy measures aimed at adjusting the balance of payments. External measures such as import quotas, tariffs, and exchange restrictions may suppress the demand for imports, but they do so at the expense of productivity and efficiency. To eliminate the excess demand, internal disinflationary measures—higher taxation and credit tightness—are necessary, and these involve the costs of reduced consumption and investment. Alternatively, the country may have to devalue its currency and incur the costs of a possible deterioration in its terms of trade, changes in in-

---

for imports via the multiplier, we also allowed for imports caused directly by the investment, the maximum expansion ratio would be correspondingly lower.

It is noteworthy that the size of the maximum expansion ratio does not depend on the type of foreign investment that is made. Even if tied loans or direct investments by subsidiaries do not involve an initial transfer problem on capital account, they may still give rise to negative transfer problems as easily as does autonomous foreign investment. Cf. Balogh and Streeten, *op. cit.*, p. 219.

come distribution, and necessary shifts of resources. When foreign investment leads to balance of payments difficulties,[19] we must include these indirect costs of a depletion of international reserves, direct controls, disinflation, or devaluation in any assessment of the benefits and costs of foreign investment.

**11.**  The costs of balance of payments adjustment are likely to be most pronounced when the borrowing country encounters the problem of debt service. Sooner or later, the outward flow of interest, dividends, and repayment of principal may exceed the rate of new borrowing. The time which elapses before this occurs will depend on the growth in new foreign borrowing, rate of interest and dividend earnings, and the amortization rate.[20] When the return flow of income and amortization payments exceeds the inflow of new loans, the country becomes a "mature debtor" and confronts a transfer problem in servicing the debt. It will have to generate an export surplus equivalent to the net outward transfer of amortization on capital account and of income payments on current account. This calls for a reallocation of resources so as to expand exports or replace imports. To accomplish this, the country may have to impose internal and external controls or experience currency depreciation, and the adverse

[19] Alternatively, it could be argued that the trouble does not stem from the foreign investment *per se*, but rather from the failure of domestic economic policy to prevent excessive investment financed by inflationary means. Nonetheless, it may be the capital inflow that stimulates additional domestic investment and adds to inflationary pressures, or at least puts pressure on existing fiscal and monetary controls of inflation. Cf. H. W. Arndt, "Overseas Borrowing—The New Model," *Economic Record*, August, 1957, pp. 252-254.

[20] An exact statement of this problem is given by E. D. Domar, "The Effect of Foreign Investment on the Balance of Payments," *American Economic Review*, December, 1950, pp. 805-826.

effects of these measures of balance of payments adjustment must then be considered as indirect costs of foreign investment, to be added to the direct costs of the foreign payments.

The direct costs of foreign debt service, however, should not in themselves be a cause for concern. True, part of the increased production from the use of foreign capital has to be paid abroad in profits or interest—and this is a deduction which would not be necessary if the savings were provided at home. But this is merely to say that the country must not expect to get an income from savings if it does not make the savings.[21] What is significant, is that the country does have additional investment, and the benefits from this may exceed the direct costs of the foreign savings that made possible the accumulation of additional capital.

Of prime concern should be the avoidance of the indirect costs of the foreign capital—the need to institute measures of balance of payments adjustment in order to find sufficient foreign exchange for the remittance of the external service payments. To escape, or at least minimize, these indirect costs, a development program should give heed to the debt servicing capacity of the country.

This becomes part of the problem of selecting appropriate investment criteria. When a development program has a high component of government investment and depends on external financing, the criteria for allocating capital must acknowledge the effects of investment on the balance of payments. This consideration, however, relates more to the choice of the pattern of goods to be produced than to the problem of technological choice in producing a particular good.[22]

[21] Cf. Hicks, *op. cit.*, p. 191.
[22] Cf. A. K. Sen, *Choice of Techniques,* Basil Blackwell, 1960, chap. VI.

To provide for adequate servicing of the foreign debt, the allocation of investment must fulfill two requirements. First, the capital should raise productivity sufficiently to yield an increase in real income greater than the interest and amortization charges. If this is done, the economy will have the capacity to raise the necessary funds—either through a direct commercial return or an increase in taxable capacity. Second, to provide a sufficient surplus of foreign exchange to avoid a transfer problem, the capital should be utilized in such a way as to generate a surplus in the other items of the balance of payments equal to the transfer payments abroad. The total supply of foreign exchange, including gross capital inflow and net use of foreign exchange reserves, must exceed the value of imports of goods and services by the amount of service payments on the foreign debt.

The creation of an export surplus also depends, of course, on the policy of the creditor country. Although we are concentrating on the debtor's position, it is obvious that the servicing problem will be easier when the creditor follows a more expansionary domestic policy and a more liberal commercial policy.

To the extent that these policies help to maintain imports from the poor country, the cyclical problem of "overborrowing" will also be mitigated. If short-run fluctuations result in a fall in export receipts for the poor country, the burden of debt servicing becomes heavier as the ratio of aggregate service payments to total foreign exchange receipts rises. This investment service ratio can be held down, however, if importing countries maintain their demand for the borrowing country's exports and if the lending countries provide capital at lower interest, for longer terms and with more stability.

The requirement for the payment of debt service can also be stated in terms of the relationship between total resource availabilities and uses.[23] If an economy is to make service payments of a certain amount in any year, it is necessary that the output produced plus capital inflow, including any net use of foreign exchange reserves, should exceed domestic consumption and investment by that amount. Or, stated in terms of the saving and investment equation, the requirement is that domestic saving plus foreign capital inflow must exceed domestic investment by the amount of debt service payments.

In the light of these requirements, it is apparent that a country's capacity to service foreign capital cannot be determined without taking into account the country's development program as a whole. Reference to the entire program is necessary for an appraisal of the conditions under which the competing claims on total resources, on saving, and on foreign exchange can be adjusted so as to release the amount required for debt service.

Moreover, the effects of a specific investment project on the balance of payments cannot be considered only from the standpoint of the particular sector to which the investment is directed: the development of one sector may influence the development of other sectors, and the balance of payments effects of any given investment will then depend on the spatial and temporal interdependence of other investments. The effects will also depend on the mobility of the factors of production and the economy's capacity to reallocate resources into export and import-competing sectors. The greater is this transforming capacity, the more indirect, but no less im-

[23] Cf. G. M. Alter, "The Servicing of Foreign Capital Inflows by Underdeveloped Countries," H. S. Ellis, ed., *Economic Development for Latin America*, St. Martin's Press, 1961, p. 140.

These fundamental relationships between the national income accounts and foreign exchange accounts have been discussed in Chapter 4 and in section 3, above.

portant, will be the balance of payments effects of a specific investment project.

Once we appreciate the relationship between total re- source availablities and uses, the interdependence of invest- ments, and the transforming capacity of the economy, we can perceive that the transfer problem can still be solved without stipulating that the investment of foreign capital should create its own means of payment by directly expand- ing exports or replacing imports. If it is realized that the ability to create a sufficiently large export surplus depends on the operation of all industries together, not simply on the use made of foreign investment alone, it is then apparent that a project financed by foreign borrowing need not itself make a direct contribution to the balance of payments.[24] In- stead of such a narrow balance of payments criterion, the basic test for the allocation of foreign capital is simply that it should be invested in the form that yields the highest social marginal product. As long as capital is distributed according to its most productive use and the excess spending associated with inflation is avoided, the necessary export surplus can be created indirectly. Even in the event that the investment yields an additional output of goods for only the home market, this will still be indirectly import-reducing—provided it does not involve inflationary financing. For the sale of the

---

[24] A similar view was taken in Chapter 4, section 5, above. Nurkse's statement of this point is worth quoting: "When additional capital be- comes available to a country, the country will want or should be urged to invest it in the form that yields the highest possible return, taking into account any external economies created by the project as well as the direct commercial yield. On the other hand, the particular goods through which the interest is transferred abroad are determined by the scale of comparative costs in international trade (though this scale need not be regarded as fixed and may well change as a result of the investment itself). No particular relation is required between the mar- ginal-productivity-of-capital schedule and the comparative-cost sched- ule." Ragnar Nurkse, *op. cit.*, pp. 136-137.

new products on the domestic market will necessarily divert expenditure away from imports. It may also indirectly increase export capacity or foster the production of import substitutes by freeing resources from other uses for transference to export or import-competing industries, providing a hitherto unavailable necessary input, lowering the cost of an input, or by yielding external economies.

The essential point, therefore, is that the allocation of foreign capital according to the criterion of productivity will also be the most favorable for debt servicing, since it maximizes the increase in income from a given amount of capital, thereby contributing to the growth of foreign exchange availabilities.

12. A final conclusion on whether the benefits of foreign investment outweigh its costs can not be reached solely in quantitative terms. Although the direct benefits and costs may be capable of quantitative assessment, it is impossible to measure all the indirect benefits and costs. Qualitative considerations must therefore enter into any final judgment on the contribution of foreign capital.

Clearly, we must avoid the extremes of either overrating or underrating the potential contribution of foreign investment to a development program. Undue optimism may come from disregarding the indirect costs of overseas borrowing and the need for complementary domestic policies in order to ensure that the external financing actually becomes an efficient means of capital formation. On the other hand, there is little justification for the view that since there are direct and indirect costs attached to an inflow of capital, it will be better to forego the foreign borrowing rather than incur the costs. This is to overlook the benefits from foreign investment and the likelihood that the benefits exceed the costs.

Instead of simply reflecting an attitude of either easy op-

timism or undue skepticism, the policies undertaken by the
borrowing country should be more discriminating among the
various forms and uses of overseas capital by attempting to
minimize the costs of foreign borrowing and making the
benefits outweigh the drawbacks as much as possible. To
gain the greatest possible contribution from foreign capital,
a development program should incorporate policies that will
stimulate a larger and more stable inflow of foreign capital,
attract foreign investment in its most desired forms, and
achieve the most effective utilization of international financing. Although specific policies cannot be formulated here
without factual studies of the particular conditions in each
country, we can at least recognize some of the major considerations that may shape these policies.

If the receipt of foreign investment does not compete with
domestic investment, and if the country adopts other measures to reduce the costs of foreign borrowing, a poor country
can undertake a more extensive development program when
a larger volume of foreign investment adds to its available
market supplies. While capital-supplying countries may
adopt some measures to stimulate foreign investment, the
policies of the borrowing country are likely to be much more
influential. Of greater consequence than the tax credits and
guarantees against certain risks that the lending country can
give, are the policies that the developing country can undertake to remove the obstacles to foreign investment. These
may range from specific measures, such as tax benefits or
Industrial Encouragement Laws, to broader policies of providing public overhead facilities, restraining inflation, and
removing foreign exchange controls and quantitative restrictions.

The recipient country should be concerned with not only
the volume of foreign investment but also with receiving

foreign investment in its most desired forms. What are the "most desired forms" depends on an assessment of the relative advantages and disadvantages of the various forms of foreign investment—not simply in the narrow context of debt servicing, but more broadly in terms of the various effects on the country's entire development program. Institutional and legal arrangements may then be designed to encourage the best combination of different types of foreign investment.[25] In formulating its investment policy, the recipient country should go beyond the traditional forms of foreign investment and consider the potentialities of newer kinds, such as joint international business ventures and management contracts for private investment, and possible approaches for transnational cooperation in providing public investment. A "partnership" arrangement in which private foreign capital is associated with local private or public capital is an especially promising device for encouraging and protecting private international investment, and for stimulating local private investment. Special attention must be given also to the particular combination of public and private borrowing to ensure that the two sources of financing are complementary rather than competitive.

While the volume of capital imports is influential in maintaining a higher level of national expenditure, the allocation of the foreign capital is decisive in determining whether it

[25] This is not an appropriate place for a thorough consideration of the institutional and legal arrangements needed to accomplish these objectives; for detailed information and analysis of different possible measures, reference may be made to W. G. Friedmann and George Kalmanoff, eds., *Joint International Business Ventures,* Columbia University Press, 1961; Southwestern Legal Foundation, *Proceedings of the 1959 Institute on Private Investments Abroad,* Matthew Bender & Co., 1959; W. G. Friedmann and R. C. Pugh, eds., *Legal Aspects of Foreign Investment,* Little, Brown, & Co., 1959.

contributes as much as possible to raising the growth-potentiality of the borrowing economy. To achieve the most effective utilization of foreign investment, the national regulation of foreign capital must be undertaken in terms of the country's entire development program—not simply on the basis of single investment projects. A program approach, not a project approach, must determine the criteria of productive use of foreign capital.[26] To realize a more efficient allocation of investment resources in terms of its entire development program, the borrowing country may have to adopt policies, such as preferential tax treatment or other incentives, that will attract private foreign investment into those sectors of the economy where it will have the maximum catalytic effect of mobilizing additional national effort. Policies affecting the allocation of foreign capital should therefore look beyond merely the direct increase in income resulting from the investment and other such short-term criteria, to the broader and long-run possibilities—from the widening of investment opportunities to even the instigating of social and cultural transformations.

In the final appraisal, all policy considerations must heed the dictum that "capital is made at home,"[27] and the basic principle that "the productivity of investment, within a single nation, is largely a matter of its external environment; it has a connexion, which is usually a close connexion, with the gains from trade."[28] Since the effective utilization of foreign capital is highly dependent on the borrowing country's ability and willingness to adopt complementary domestic policies,

[26] Cf. P. N. Rosenstein-Rodan, "International Aid for Underdeveloped Countries," *Review of Economics and Statistics,* May, 1961, pp. 107-108.
[27] Nurkse, *Problems of Capital Formation in Underdeveloped Countries, op. cit.,* p. 141.
[28] Hicks, *op. cit.,* p. 180.

there can be no simple equivalence between the amount of the country's foreign borrowing and its rate of development. In determining whether development is to be sustained over the longer run, the use made of the foreign capital in terms of the country's entire development program will be more decisive than the initial volume of foreign investment.

# 6   *Commercial Policy*

**1.** Commercial policy comprises another major area of international economic policy that should be reconsidered in the light of development programming. This raises the controversial issue of whether the traditional case for free trade —convincing as it may be on the grounds of maximizing world production efficiency under static conditions—is directly relevant for the structural and dynamic problems of poor nations. In general terms, it may be asked whether free trade is the optimal policy when the conditions of production efficiency are considered on an inter-temporal basis, instead of for only a single time period, and when the concern is with national gains, instead of mutual gains from trade. More pointedly, it may be contended that a protective commercial policy will strengthen a development program by enabling the poor country to acquire a larger share of the gains from trade, increase its rate of capital formation, and promote its industrialization.[1] In support of these contentions, several specific arguments favoring a protective commercial policy might be advocated. This chapter appraises the analytical validity of these arguments and their relevance for development programming.

2.    The belief that a poor country can alter the distribution of the gains from trade in its favor, and thereby directly raise its real income, is based on the terms of trade argument for protection. An expected deterioration in their terms of trade is a common concern of poor countries. This expectation rests partly on an extrapolation of the alleged secular deterioration in their terms of trade, and partly on a belief that future improvements in primary production, together with a low income elasticity of demand for primary products will lower the prices of the poor country's exports relative to its imports.[2] It is argued that a tariff that restricts exports or imports, and results in a rise in export prices or a fall in import prices, may forestall the anticipated deterioration or may bring about an improvement in the terms of trade.

The logic of this argument is that a country need not act as

[1] The inappropriateness of relying on commercial policy to maintain external balance has already been discussed in Chapter 4.

The possibility of using commercial policy to offset fluctuations in foreign exchange income is not considered here. Even though cyclical fluctuations in export receipts may affect the rate and pattern of a country's development, their adverse effects are more appropriately met by stability measures than by protective trade policies. Some stability measures are suggested in Chapter 7, section 10.

Nor do we give any emphasis to the possibilities of using commercial policy to alter the internal distribution of income. Analytically interesting as this argument is, the redistribution effects of a tariff are not likely to have much practical bearing on the rate of development.

[2] Cf. Raúl Prebisch, "Commercial Policy in the Underdeveloped Countries," *American Economic Review, Papers and Proceedings*, May, 1959, pp. 261-264.

a perfect competitor, but may instead impose a tariff that makes its *marginal* terms of trade (marginal receipts or marginal revenue) equal to its marginal rate of transformation (marginal costs), in contrast to the free trade situation in which the terms of trade (that is, the *price* of exports in terms of imports) are equated to the marginal rate of transformation (Fig. 2).[3] If the trade-controlling country can exploit a monopoly or monopsony position, it can trade on better terms by restricting its volume of trade.

Although this argument is analytically valid, as was recognized by classical economists, its practical relevance for poor countries may be only slight. Few, if any, of these countries can exercise sufficient monopoly or monopsony power—especially in view of alternative sources of supply for foodstuffs on the part of importing countries, the capacity of advanced industrial nations to develop synthetics as substitutes for natural raw materials, and the relatively small size of any one poor country's domestic market for a particular import. A tariff is most effective in improving the tariff-imposing country's terms of trade when the foreign offer curve is inelastic,[4]

[3] Gottfried Haberler, *A Survey of International Trade Theory*, International Finance Section, Princeton University, revised edition, 1961, p. 53; James E. Meade, *Trade and Welfare*, Oxford University Press, 1955, chap. XVII.

[4] It is sometimes argued that a tariff will at one and the same time improve the terms of trade, protect import-competing industries, and raise the real earnings of the factor used relatively intensively in producing importables. If, however, the foreign offer curve is inelastic, these objectives are likely to be contradictory. For then the terms of trade may improve so much that the domestic price of imports falls in the tariff-imposing country, with a consequent reduction in the domestic production of importables and a redistribution of earned income towards the factor used relatively intensively in producing exportables. Cf. Harry G. Johnson, "Income Distribution, The Offer Curve, and the Effects of Tariffs," *Manchester School of Economic and Social Studies*, September, 1960, pp. 223-224, 230-232; L. A. Metzler, "Tariffs, the

but the foreign offer curve that confronts any single poor
country will normally be elastic, with less imports being demanded and less exports supplied as the price of imports
rises. The greater is this elasticity, the more will the volume
of trade decrease as a result of a tariff. The problem then
becomes one of calculating the optimal tariff rate, or more
precisely, the optimal import and export duties. An optimal
import or export duty is one that maximizes the gain from
improved terms of trade minus the loss from a smaller volume
of trade; and this duty will be lower, the greater is the elasticity of the foreign offer curve.

However, even if we assume the existence of sufficient
monopoly or monopsony power, and ignore the practical
difficulties of calculating an optimal tariff, the terms of trade
argument is still limited severely by its dependence on price-
elasticities of demand and supply at only a given moment of
time. The conclusion may be quite different if it is recognized
that a short-term gain may be easily offset by subsequent
changes in elasticities. It is also possible for an initial improvement to be later counteracted by the retaliation of other
countries, by an increased demand for imports occasioned by
the government's expenditure of the tariff proceeds, or an
internal redistribution of income. If these dynamic effects are
not taken into account, the terms of trade argument may be
misleading, and may be given more weight than it merits in
the context of development.

3.  The second category of protection arguments concen-

Terms of Trade and the Distribution of National Income," *Journal of
Political Economy,* February, 1949, pp. 1-29. Metzler notes in particular that if a primary producing country faces an inelastic foreign
demand, it may not succeed in either stimulating domestic manufacturing or raising labor's share of income by imposing a tariff. *Ibid.,*
pp. 19-28.

trates on the need to increase investment. An improvement in the terms of trade can be one source of capital formation if the extra income is saved, but there are also other means by which commercial policy can contribute to capital accumulation.

One way is by increasing the savings ratio through controls on imports of consumer goods. The objective of greater investment will not be realized, however, if consumption expenditure merely shifts from imports to domestic products. A reduction in consumption expenditure—not a mere change in its composition—is needed for an increase in saving.

This requirement applies even if the importation of consumer goods is controlled in order to be replaced directly by imports of capital goods. Only if there is also a corresponding act of domestic saving will the new capital imports be a net contribution to capital formation. If the import restrictions do not lead to a reduction in consumers' expenditure, but simply to a switch of spending from imported consumer goods to domestic commodities, the increase in home consumption will draw domestic factors away from capital construction or maintenance. Home consumption simply rises at the expense of domestic investment, and the imports of capital goods are offset by the reduced domestic investment, so that there is no increase in total net capital formation. Barring an increase in voluntary saving, an increase in net investment could then come about only through the forced saving that results from inflation when the local purchase of imported capital goods is financed through domestic credit expansion.

The effectiveness of protection as a means of increasing investment is thus contingent upon a complementary domestic policy of mobilizing additional saving. Even if import restrictions allow more imports of capital goods in place of consumption goods, it is ultimately an increase in voluntary or compulsory saving that makes for the net contribution to capital formation.[5]

In connection with this argument, proponents of import controls frequently maintain that import restrictions will not reduce the total volume of imports but only alter their composition from consumer goods to capital goods. But this assumes that protection has no adverse effects on exports. In practice, the protection of import-competing industries tends to attract resources away from other industries, including export industries. Unless the protected industries draw away only the disguised unemployed, exports will then be handicapped. Insofar as the extent of disguised unemployment tends to be exaggerated,[6] this is a real possibility. Consideration must also be given to the fact that for peasants who have the alternative of subsistence production or production of cash crops for export, the incentive to produce export crops may be highly dependent upon an aspiration to consume imported goods. The denial of imports may then reduce the incentive of peasants to produce for the market. Moreover, when the policies of protection and promotion of import-competing industries result in higher internal costs, the maintenance of exports becomes extremely difficult. Even if they are not directly designed to do so, the import restrictions may thus have adverse indirect repercussions on exports and result in a reduced capacity to import, although only a change in the composition of imports was intended.

4. The foregoing argument relates to an increase in the do-

[5] This basic principle has been emphasized by Ragnar Nurkse, *Problems of Capital Formation in Underdeveloped Countries*, Basil Blackwell, 1953, pp. 112-116.
[6] See section 8, below.

mestic savings ratio, but protection may also be advocated as a means of capital formation through its attraction of foreign investment. A general proposition of neoclassical trade theory is that commodity movements are a substitute for international factor movements. Protection may then stimulate factor movements in place of commodity trade, since protection has the effect of increasing the relative scarcity of the scarce factor in the tariff-imposing country, thereby raising the factor's real return and making profitable an international redistribution of the factor.

Accordingly, for a poor country in which capital is the scarce factor, a tariff imposed on a capital-intensive industry may induce an inflow of foreign capital.[7] When the tariff is imposed, the price of the capital-intensive product rises relatively to the price of the labor-intensive product, and factors move out of the labor-intensive industry into the capital-intensive industry. There will then be, at constant factor prices, an excess supply of labor and an excess demand for capital. The marginal product of labor must therefore fall, and the marginal product of capital must rise.[8] In response to this higher marginal product of capital in the capital-poor country, capital may then be attracted from the capital-rich country where marginal products have remained constant.

This argument depends, however, on several restrictive assumptions. It assumes that production functions are iden-

---

[7] This argument is analyzed fully by R. A. Mundell, "International Trade and Factor Mobility," *American Economic Review*, June, 1957, pp. 331-335.

[8] In the case of a tariff on a capital-intensive industry, the ratios of labor to capital rise in both the capital-intensive and labor-intensive industries. If the production functions are subject to constant returns to scale, then the marginal productivities of factors depend only on factor proportions, so that in this situation the marginal product of capital rises and the marginal product of labor falls.

tical in all countries, and that capital is perfectly mobile and will respond to a change in marginal product. But differences in production functions are undoubtedly pronounced between poor and rich countries; because of these differences, the tariff may not make capital movements profitable. It is also unrealistic to ignore other determinants of foreign investment besides a differential in the return on capital. The argument also precludes any change in the terms of trade. If, however, the tariff should improve the terms of trade, the price of the labor-intensive export commodity may increase relatively to the capital-intensive import commodity, and the marginal product of capital would then not rise.

Even if all the assumptions are granted, and capital does move until its marginal product is equal in both countries, the tariff will still have unfavorable effects which the capital movement at best can only alleviate, but not eliminate. As a result of the tariff, the marginal product of labor will fall, and real wages will be lower than in the pretariff situation. This is because the capital inflow will be largely absorbed in an expansion of the output of capital-intensive importables and can never succeed in raising the capital-labor ratio in each industry to its pretariff level. Only if the assumption of constant returns to scale is replaced by an assumption that external economies of scale exist in the production of capital-intensive importables, so that the marginal product of capital falls at a slower rate than it would in the absence of such economies, would it be possible for the tariff to attract a sufficiently greater supply of capital to allow the new equilibrium to be established with a higher marginal product of labor.[9]

A less sophisticated but more realistic case for protection as a means of attracting foreign investment is simply the old-

[9] Mundell, *op. cit.*, pp. 333-334.

fashioned appeal for "tariff factories." When a poor country imposes prohibitive tariffs, or other import restrictions, against foreign manufacturers, the inflow of direct foreign investment may increase as the foreign manufacturer is induced to escape the import controls by establishing a branch plant or subsidiary behind the tariff wall. Although the protection may not be effective in attracting supply-oriented industries, it may appeal to market-oriented industries. It may particularly encourage the final stages of manufacture and assembly of parts within the tariff-imposing country when there is an import duty on finished products while raw materials or parts remain untaxed. But the tariff alone can not ensure a sufficiently high domestic demand for the product of the tariff factory; as long as the domestic market for the restricted import remains narrow, the necessary condition for the attraction of direct foreign investment will not be fulfilled. If, however, a former supplier of an import can be induced by the protection to come in and establish an industry behind the tariff, this may be the easiest way in which the country can gain not only capital, but also the technical knowledge and experience that are so necessary for the successful establishment of a new industry. The attraction of foreign capital, entrepreneurs, and skilled immigrants will be even more beneficial to the host country if it can attract the outside firm on terms that will enable the participation of local capital and enterprise, as in joint international business ventures. Such forms of partnership association may even provide for an increasing degree of participation by national interests over time.

**5.** We may now examine the advocacy of protection in order to accelerate the industrialization of poor countries. Gunnar Myrdal makes a challenging case for protection by maintaining that there are "four special reasons for industrial protection in underdeveloped countries—the difficulties of finding demand to match new supply, the existence of surplus labor, the large rewards of individual investments in creating external economies, and the lopsided internal price structure disfavoring industry."[10] These reasons are interrelated and may be interpreted as an extension of the infant industry argument to the "growing up" of the economy as a whole. In combination, they constitute an "infant economy" case for protection, and as such they have considerable appeal to a poor country. Nonetheless, a closer investigation of the arguments may temper this enthusiasm if it is realized that to be a guide to policy, the protection argument must be not only logically valid, but also supported by empirical evidence, not offset by practical qualifications, and superior to alternative domestic policies.

These other considerations limit the significance of even the time-honored infant industry argument. Temporary tariff protection of an infant industry is supported on grounds that the existing comparative cost relations are irrelevant, insofar as after a certain period of time the initial production difficulties will have been overcome through practice, and the industry will then be able to produce at lower costs, through the full exploitation of economies of scale. The industry will thereby eventually acquire a comparative advantage.

This is a logically acceptable argument, but the scope of its applicability may be rather narrow. At best, the tariff can only be an instrument for channeling resources into specific industries; but it cannot create the capital or skills required by the industry at the outset. Before an industry can be pro-

[10] Gunnar Myrdal, *An International Economy*, Harper & Brothers, 1956, p. 279.

tected, it must first be created.[11] Assuming, however, that this prior problem has been solved, the protected industry must still meet not only the "Mill test" of acquiring sufficient skill and experience to overcome an historical handicap, but also a "Bastable test" of realizing a sufficient saving in costs to compensate for the high costs of the learning period.[12] It is also necessary to be sure that the industry would not expand except with the aid of a tariff. On this basis, the case for a protective tariff is weak if there are only internal economies of scale—not external economies. For, even though there may be losses on early operations, if the future scale of output is sufficient to enable the current rate of interest to be earned on the initial amount invested in learning the job, the investment will be profitable for private enterprise. The justification for state support is slight when there are simply costs of growth as such; the case is only strong when the expansion of the industry leads to external economies and thereby a divergence between private and social costs.[13]

Even if we are cognizant of these requirements, the cor-

[11] Nurkse, *op. cit.*, p. 105; A. O. Hirschman, *The Strategy of Economic Development*, Yale University Press, 1958, p. 124. An essential conclusion of Hirschman's analysis of commercial policy is that infant industry protection should not be given before the industry has been established, but should become available, if at all, only afterwards.

[12] M. C. Kemp, "The Mill-Bastable Infant-Industry Dogma," *Journal of Political Economy*, February, 1960, pp. 65-67.

[13] Meade, *op. cit.*, pp. 256-257, 270-271. This restrictive condition may appear unnecessarily extreme, however, when the profitability of an investment project is delayed for an especially long period, so that the risk element is particularly great for the individual investor and the degree of individual time-preference is unduly high, as compared with what may be appropriate from the point of view of the community. Cf. William Fellner, "Individual Investment Projects in Growing Economies," *Investment Criteria and Economic Growth*, Center for International Studies, Massachusetts Institute of Technology, 1955, pp. 125-130.

rect selection of genuine infant industries remains uncertain, insofar as it entails forecasting changes in cost conditions and the magnitude of future external economies. Instead of trying to impose selective tariffs of sufficient height to encourage particular industries, it may therefore be more expedient to place a uniform *ad valorem* tariff on the whole range of industrial products and then leave the selection to market forces.[14] This would avoid the overreaching of import substitution into all lines and would still allow specialization according to comparative advantage. For even if it were true that disguised unemployment in agriculture makes production in accordance with comparative cost inapplicable at the margin between agricultural and industrial production, comparative advantage should still apply between one industrial product and another.

**6.** Turning now from cost conditions to demand conditions, we may consider the proposal that protection is needed to create demand to match new supply. Whereas the infant industry argument maintains that the industry's present costs are too high, it might also be claimed that the demand for its product is too low, and that "one of the difficulties of industrial development in underdeveloped countries, and one of the great hindrances to giving real momentum to a development policy, is that internal demand must be built up simultaneously with supply."[15] It is thus argued that the unlikelihood, or "the exasperating slowness of any self-engendered process of 'natural growth' " calls for import restrictions that "afford a means of by-passing altogether this process of

[14] Cf. Nicholas Kaldor, "Conferências sôbre desenvolvimento econômica," *Revista Brasileira de Economia,* March, 1957, pp. 28-29.
[15] Myrdal, *op. cit.,* p. 276.

'natural growth' and creating at once the necessary demand for a particular domestic industry."[16]

As stated, this argument is restricted simply to promoting the demand for import substitutes. Yet, aside from foreign exchange restrictions, there is no indication why this drive for self-sufficiency is preferable to any alternative pattern of development. Even if the argument is extended to the "balanced growth" thesis, the particular emphasis on import-substitutes is unwarranted. For the balanced growth doctrine, as formulated by Nurkse, calls only for a balanced pattern of investment in a number of different industries, including agriculture, so that people working with more capital and better techniques become each other's customers. It does not emphasize import-competing industries, and there is nothing in the doctrine itself to favor general protection for industry as contrasted with other policies designed to promote extensive investment. Indeed, Nurkse cautions that import restrictions should be used only sparingly, because they lead to costly and inefficient import-substitute production and have an adverse effect on real income. Further, Nurkse carefully stresses that the case for output expansion for the home market is clear only on the condition that the amount of resources is increasing at a sufficient rate—through population growth, capital accumulation, and the spread of knowledge—so that domestic output can expand without neglecting export production and giving up the benefits achieved through international specialization.[17]

[16] Loc. cit.

[17] Ragnar Nurkse, "International Trade Theory and Development Policy," Howard S. Ellis, ed., Economic Development for Latin America, St. Martin's Press, 1961, pp. 251-254, 257-258; "The Conflict between 'Balanced Growth' and International Specialization," Lectures on Economic Development, Faculty of Economics, Istanbul University, 1958, pp. 177-180; Patterns of Trade and Development, Wicksell

Finally, it should be recognized that import restrictions are designed merely to replace imports—but this in itself is no guarantee of cumulative growth beyond the point that imports have been replaced. The problems involved in sustaining the development momentum may be quite different from those of initiating development, and other policies may be more appropriate to achieve a self-sustaining process of development.

7.   A more cogent argument for industrial protection is that the establishment or expansion of an industry will yield external economies, thereby giving rise to a divergence between social and private returns. This divergence is of especial concern to a poor country in connection with the problem of allocating savings among alternative investment opportunities. The market evaluation of comparative advantage may not conform to the investment criterion of social profitability,[18] and governmental support of the industry that yields external economies may then be advocated to correct the market mechanism.

Neoclassicists recognized that as an industry's scale of out-

Lectures, Almquist & Wiksell, 1959, pp. 41-48 (reprinted in *Equilibrium and Growth in the World Economy. Economic Essays by Ragnar Nurkse*, Harvard University Press, 1961, pp. 314-322).

[18] To meet this problem, the linear programming approach to development planning attempts to include a number of non-market (but quantifiable) phenomena by using accounting prices in evaluating the allocation of resources. By this method, the optimal pattern of trade is determined simultaneously with the optimal allocation of investment. This approach does not, however, necessarily support protection; it may show that the country's development policies are actually over-emphasizing import-substitution and neglecting the potential gains from trade. For a detailed discussion, see Hollis B. Chenery, "Comparative Advantage and Development Policy," *American Economic Review*, March, 1961, pp. 33-48.

put expanded, the firms within the industry might benefit from a shift downward in their cost curves as a result of "external technological effects." These external technological economies affect the firm's output via changes in its production function.[19] If the price of the product of the expanding industry falls as its output increases, firms in other industries which use the product of the expanding industry as an input will also realize lower production costs; this may be termed an "external pecuniary economy," and will affect the firm's profits.[20]

If production costs are lowered for firms in other industries, for technical or pecuniary reasons, as the result of an expansion in output of the protected industry, the social cost is less than the private cost of production. In this situation, private profitability understates the social desirability of an expansion of the protected industry; market forces would lead to a less than optimal output of commodities whose production involves external economies. Or, if investment in one sector increases the profitability of investment in another sector via increases in demand, market forces will again not necessarily lead to optimal investment decisions.

External economies are commonly believed to be more im-

[19] Cf. Jacob Viner, "Cost Curves and Supply Curves," reprinted in American Economic Association, *Readings in Price Theory*, Richard D. Irwin, Inc., 1952, pp. 217-220; James E. Meade, "External Economies and Diseconomies in a Competitive Situation," *Economic Journal*, March, 1952, pp. 54-67.

[20] T. Scitovsky, "Two Concepts of External Economies," *Journal of Political Economy*, April, 1954, pp. 146-151. The lowering of production costs is only one of the possible instances of pecuniary external economies. As Scitovsky notes, expansion in industry A may also give rise to profits (1) in an industry that produces a factor used in industry A, (2) in an industry whose product is complementary in use to the product of industry A, (3) in an industry whose product is a substitute for a factor used in industry A, or (4) in an industry whose product is consumed by persons whose incomes are raised by the expansion of industry A.

portant in the industrial sectors than in primary production, so that their omission from the market mechanism is likely to bias resource allocation against manufacturing.[21] The argument of external economies, as related to a poor country, might therefore be broadened to support general protection for industry by claiming that the profitability of any single industry is a function of the total number and diversity of industries in the economy. Cost reductions in a single industry may be especially dependent upon the economies of conglomeration when a large number of industries are all "conglomerated" close together in the same locality.[22] More generally, interindustry external economies may stem from the complementarity of industries on the side of costs, reinforcing the "balanced growth" doctrine which stresses complementarity on the side of demand. [23] By supporting these interindustry relationships, protection to facilitate the growth of a range of industries or an entire industrial complex may then allow each industry to become profitable, whereas investment in each of the separate industries considered in isolation might be unprofitable.

Although the external economies argument is formally correct, modern proponents of protection are less careful to qualify it than were the neoclassicists.[24] Myrdal, for instance, believes that external economies are realizable in import-competing industries, and he is sanguine about the govern-

[21] Cf. Chenery, *op. cit.*, pp. 20-25.

[22] Meade, *Trade and Welfare, op. cit.*, p. 258.

[23] Cf. Jacob Viner, "Stability and Progress: The Poorer Countries' Problem," D. C. Hague, ed., *Stability and Progress*, St. Martin's Press, 1958, pp. 56-57.

These interactions are also related to the "linkages" discussed by Hirschman, *op. cit.*, chap. 6.

[24] Cf. Alfred Marshall, *Principles of Economics*, eighth edition, Macmillan & Co., 1920, pp. 226, 271, 317-318, 615, 808; Allyn Young, "Increasing Returns and Economic Progress," *Economic Journal*, December, 1928, pp. 528 ff.; Jacob Viner, *Studies in the Theory of*

ment's ability to estimate these external economies within a
dynamic "national calculus."[25] Actually, what is essential is
a calculation of the *net* external economies—that is, gross
external economies *minus* external diseconomies—for all possible *alternative* investment opportunities. Insofar as investment funds are limited in any development program, the
emphasis on import-competing industries must depend on an
assumption that the net external economies realizable are
greatest in import-competing industries. There is, however,
no *a priori* reason why this should be so; external economies
might be substantial in the export sector, or domestic industries, or in public overhead capital.

It is also necessary to distinguish whether the external
economies are reversible or irreversible—that is, whether the
gains to other enterprises continue even after protection is
withdrawn and output in the formerly protected enterprise
is reduced. For, if they are reversible, the protection must
then be permanent, rather than merely temporary, to keep
the reversible external economies utilized. The case of irreversible external economies can be considered as merging
with the infant industry situation, but this does not apply to
reversible external economies.

8. Finally, it is claimed that protection of industry in a poor
country is justified because the structure of internal costs and
prices tends to be lopsided between industry and agriculture

---

*International Trade,* Harper & Brothers, 1937, pp. 480-482; H. S.
Ellis and W. Fellner, "External Economies and Diseconomies," *American Economic Review,* September, 1943, pp. 493-511; Meade, *Trade
and Welfare, op. cit.,* chap. XVI; Marcus Fleming, "External Economies and the Doctrine of Balanced Growth," *Economic Journal,* June,
1955, pp. 241-256; H. W. Arndt, "External Economies in Economic
Growth," *Economic Record,* November, 1955, pp. 192-214.

[25] Myrdal, *op. cit.,* pp. 276-277.

in a way that disfavors industry. An early version of this argument was stated by Manoilesco who maintained that the advantage of international trade exists only for industrial countries—identified as the rich countries—and not for countries whose imports consist of industrial articles and whose exports are agricultural products—identified as the poor countries.[26] Believing that industry is superior to agriculture as shown by a great difference between the average income per head of an agricultural worker and that of an industrial worker, Manoilesco advocated protection to facilitate the transfer of workers from low-productivity agriculture to high-productivity industry. Myrdal and others restate the argument in modern form: they claim there is a wide gap in real wages between industry and agriculture, but that the social costs for labor in industry are actually lower than the money wages. They therefore advocate trade controls to compensate for the gap in labor costs between industry and agriculture.[27]

In a more rigorous fashion, Professor Hagen demonstrates that when there are large differentials in factor returns in different sectors because of imperfect factor markets or the use of different factor proportions, real income can be increased by factor redistribution.[28] If the distortion in factor allocation is removed by protecting the industry with the higher factor price, real income will be raised relatively to

[26]Mihail Manoilesco, *Theory of Protection and International Trade*, English edition, P. S. King, 1931. Also, cf. Bertil Ohlin, "Protection and Non-Competing Groups," *Weltwirtschaftliches Archiv*, 1931, pp. 30-45.

[27] Myrdal, *op. cit.*, pp. 277-278; W. A. Lewis, "Economic Development with Unlimited Supplies of Labour," *Manchester School of Economic and Social Studies*, May, 1954, pp. 185-186.

[28] E. E. Hagen, "An Economic Justification of Protectionism," *Quarterly Journal of Economics*, November, 1958, pp. 496-514.

the free trade situation—provided that the increase in the aggregate cost to buyers of the protected product is less than the increase in income to the factors which shift to the protected industry. Even then, it is suggested that if such possibilities for achieving a real comparative advantage do exist, the most desirable policy would be to combine free trade with a subsidy per unit of labor in industry, equal to the difference between the higher unit labor cost in industry and the lower labor cost in agriculture.[29]

The existence of disguised unemployment in agriculture is thought to provide a specific application of this general argument to a poor country.[30] If the concept of disguised unemployment is interpreted strictly, it means that beyond a certain number of workers the marginal productivity of labor is zero in agriculture, and that when some labor is withdrawn from agriculture, output can still be maintained without any change in organization or in cooperant factors. While the marginal product of the surplus labor is not enough for its own support, the institutional arrangement of the family farm, in which the unit of production is also the unit of consumption, allows the members of the household to share in the total product, receiving approximately the average product. When the marginal product of labor is less than the average product, the marginal workers are, in effect, being subsidized by the rest of the peasant community. Nonetheless, to induce the excess workers to transfer to industrial employment from agriculture, it is generally necessary to offer a premium above the subsistence wage in the rural sector. Although the social opportunity cost, as determined by the marginal product in agriculture is zero, the cost to industrialists of hiring the surplus labor is considerably higher. In such

[29] *Ibid.*, pp. 510-511.
[30] *Ibid.*, p. 514.

a situation, labor is overvalued for the industrial sector, and
the ratio of social cost to money cost is lower in industry than
in agriculture. It is therefore claimed that a better utilization
of domestic resources can be achieved if secondary industries
are protected in order to offset the divergence between private money costs and true social marginal costs.

This appeal to the existence of disguised unemployment
is, however, a tenuous foundation for a protection argument.
At most, disguised unemployment applies to peasant or self-
employed labor working on small farms, not to plantation
labor, and not to thinly-populated countries. It may also be
only a seasonal phenomenon: there may be no excess of labor
supply over labor requirements at the planting and harvest
seasons. Rarely is conclusive evidence offered to show that
there actually is in agriculture a substantial amount of labor
that could be released with no effect on production, if other
measures are not taken. To be sure, the measurement of disguised unemployment is difficult, but one might at least observe whether the labor resources of the poor countries
actually behave as if there were considerable unemployment.
According to Professor Schultz, experience in several countries demonstrates that "programs based on disguised unemployment have not performed as expected: instead of labor
resources responding to an increase in the money supply or
to new industries in the way that one would have expected
if there were considerable underemployment, workers act
as if the marginal productivities of laborers in agriculture and
in other fields are about the same."[31] Schultz also maintains
that he knows of no evidence for any poor country anywhere
that would suggest that a transfer of even some small frac-

[31] T. W. Schultz, *The Economic Test in Latin America*, New York
State School of Industrial and Labor Relations, Cornell University,
Bulletin 35, August, 1956, pp. 14-15.

tion, say, five percent, of the existing labor force out of agriculture, with other things equal, could be made without reducing production.[32] Several others have also questioned the notion of disguised unemployment,[33] and the earlier estimates of the amount of disguised unemployment now appear to have been exaggerated. Even Nurkse, who originally emphasized the concept of surplus farm labor, states that "much of the surplus labor that may exist in subsistence agriculture is not readily available for other uses unless it is released through changes in agricultural organization. Such changes are a major undertaking and cannot be lightly taken for granted."[34] But what is clear, and of most significance, is that the productivity of labor is generally low in all activities —non-agricultural as well as agricultural. It may therefore be

[32] T. W. Schultz, "The Role of Government in Promoting Economic Development," L. D. White, ed., *The State of the Social Sciences,* University of Chicago Press, 1956, p. 375.

[33] N. Köstner, "Comments on Professor Nurkse's Capital Accumulation in Underdeveloped Countries," *L'Egypte Contemporaine,* No. 272, 1952; Doreen Warriner, *Land Reform and Economic Development,* National Bank of Egypt, Cairo, 1955, pp. 25-26; Benjamin Higgins, "Prospects for an International Economy," *World Politics,* April, 1957, p. 466; Jacob Viner, "Some Reflections on the Concept of Disguised Unemployment," *Indian Journal of Economics,* July, 1957, pp. 17-23; Gottfried Haberler, *International Trade and Economic Development,* National Bank of Egypt, Cairo, 1959, pp. 25-27; Harry T. Oshima, "Underemployment in Backward Economies: An Empirical Comment," *Journal of Political Economy,* June, 1958, pp. 259-264.

[34] Ragnar Nurkse, "Stabilization and Development of Primary Producing Countries," *Kyklos,* 1958, pp. 261-262. Again, in his Istanbul lecture (p. 200), Nurkse maintained that "Some of the underdeveloped countries do have potential domestic resources available for capital construction. But it may be very hard for them to mobilize these resources, and it may be impossible to mobilize them without resorting to coercive methods. Even the necessary labor is not always available for construction: as a rule, it can be released from the land only through changes—and possibly revolutionary changes—in agricultural organization."

more appropriate to conclude with Professor Viner that "there is little or nothing in all the phenomena designated as 'disguised unemployment,' as 'hidden unemployment,' or as 'underemployment' which insofar as they constitute genuine social problems would not be adequately taken into account by competent, informed, and comprehensive analysis of the phenomenon of low productivity of *employed* labor, its causes, its true extent, and its possible remedies."[35]

Moreover, even assuming for argument's sake that disguised unemployment does exist, it still does not follow that industrialization through protection is the best solution. The mere existence of surplus manpower cannot be taken to mean that these individuals are either available or qualified to be permanent industrial laborers. The most significant effect of surplus labor in agriculture is low productivity, but the basic remedy for this, as Nurkse emphasizes, is capital formation, not industrialization as such.[36] Disguised unemployment constitutes simply an "investible surplus" which can be applied in various investment outlets. The labor need not be transferred from agriculture to industry, but might be better directed to other capital-formation projects.

[35] Viner, *op. cit.*, p. 23.

[36] In Nurkse's words, "Some writers argue that since the problem is *agricultural* over-population, the cure is to transfer labor from agriculture to industry. Even though industrialization is a normal consequence of development, this view is in my opinion superficial. The effect of over-population is low productivity, for which capital formation, not industrialization as such, is the basic economic remedy. In what particular fields the capital is applied depends on many things including foreign trade opportunities and domestic income elasticities of demand. Often it is the category of public overhead facilities that claims the biggest share in a poor country's investment program. Often it is here that surplus farm labor can best be used: in building roads, railroads, schools, power plants and irrigation works." Nurkse, "Excess Population and Capital Construction," *Malayan Economic Review*, October, 1957, p. 8.

Instead of resorting to offsetting tariffs, other measures might be more effective in directly stimulating labor mobility. Disguised unemployment cannot be attributed to any deficiency of demand; it is instead due to real causes such as land shortage, capital deficiency, and the lack of skills and organization which would be needed to utilize the underemployed labor in other activities.[37] When a poor country's market system is so rudimentary and its economy so inflexible, protection is unlikely to bring about the desired supply responses to price and income stimuli. When occupational mobility is restricted by institutional and cultural barriers, extra-economic measures are required. In general, labor mobility might be better encouraged by public investment in overhead capital, education and training, land tenure reforms, and other policies that remove the social and institutional barriers to mobility.

Moreover, even if the private cost in agriculture is too low because wages are depressed, and in industry the private cost is too high compared with what it would be if the disguised unemployed competed freely in the labor market, the exact opposite may exist in the capital market. It is generally true that rates of interest are considerably higher and capital is more overvalued in the agricultural sectors of poor countries than in the industrial sectors. The essential question, therefore, is whether manufacturing costs as a whole are overstated relatively to agricultural costs. This depends on the relative capital-labor ratios in the two sectors and the relative sizes of the wage and interest rate differentials between the two sectors. It is then likely that the counterbalancing effects of the higher interest rate in agriculture and the higher capital-labor ratio in industry may more than off-

[37] Cf. J. R. Hicks, *Essays in World Economics,* Oxford University Press, 1959, pp. 178-179.

set the overvaluation of labor in industry. When due attention is given to capital, it is quite possible that the ratio of social cost to private cost is higher in industry than in agriculture.

Further, the marginal productivity of capital and the capacity to absorb capital may well be greater in agriculture, because of the scarcity of complementary factors which industrial capital would require in order to be successful, especially the shortages of certain raw materials and the lack of managerial ability and labor skills. These scarcities create bottlenecks in industrial production and bring about a sharp decline in the marginal productivity of capital. Capital absorption in industry is also constrained by the need to avoid inflation and balance of payments disequilibrium.

9.  Underlying the foregoing specific qualifications to the various arguments for industrial protection is a more general criticism—protection is likely to conflict seriously with the strategic roles that agriculture and exports must have in the development process. From the experience of development programs, it has become increasingly apparent that a poor country cannot afford to neglect its agricultural base. Higher agricultural productivity is necessary to supply food for a growing population, to supply raw materials for expanding domestic industry, to create a "marketable surplus" in the agricultural sector and thereby a demand for nonagricultural commodities, to provide additional foreign exchange earnings, and to contribute to capital formation.[38] If distortions between industry and agriculture, and between the domestic

[38] The importance of agriculture's role in the process of development is clearly analyzed by B. F. Johnston and J. W. Mellor, "The Role of Agriculture in Economic Devlopment," *American Economic Review,* September, 1961, pp. 566-593.

and foreign sectors are to be avoided, agricultural development must accompany industrial development.

To forestall criticism, the proponents of protection frequently assert that protection would cause only a relative, not absolute, contraction of agricultural production, and that there would be no reduction in the volume of trade, but only a change in the composition of imports. But, as we have previously noted, this overlooks the very real likelihood that, even if it is not directly designed to do so, the emphasis on industrialization will have indirect effects that are adverse for agriculture and exports. If the limited financial and human resources of the government are concentrated on an industrialization program, if productive resources are attracted away from other sectors to the protected industries, or if the industrialization program is inflationary, then agriculture and exports will suffer. There is considerable evidence that this has happened in several development programs.[39]

The basic question therefore remains—whether, when all the direct and indirect costs of protection are evaluated, the increase in national product that is expected from the encouragement of industry will constitute a net gain. This decisive issue certainly cannot be resolved by simply claiming that "manufacturing industry represents, in a sense, a higher stage of production," or that "the productivity of manpower in industry tends to be considerably greater than in the traditional agricultural pursuits."[40] This is to beg the question

[39] T. W. Schultz, "Latin American Policy Lessons," *American Economic Review, Papers and Proceedings,* May, 1956, pp. 425-432; United Nations, Department of Economic and Social Affairs, *Processes and Problems of Industrialization in Underdeveloped Countries,* New York, 1955, pp. 72-74; Louis O. Delwart, *The Future of Latin American Exports to the United States,* National Planning Association, 1960, chap. V.

[40] Myrdal, *op. cit.,* p. 226.

by introducing an irrelevant comparison between the efficient manufacturing of an advanced country and the inefficient agriculture that presently exists in a poor country.

In itself, primary production cannot be identified as a cause of poverty; the relative concentration on primary production is merely an associative—not causative—characteristic of poverty. The high ratio of agricultural population to total population is a consequence, rather than a cause, of poverty. Where the agricultural population is poor, the non-agricultural population serving the agricultural sector will be small and also poor. Where agriculture is highly productive, the nonfarm population will be large and also prosperous.[41] Thus, since it is the low productivity in agriculture that is significant, it must be demonstrated that protectionist policies to encourage industry, rather than alternative policies to raise agricultural productivity, would result in the allocation of the poor country's scarce resources to their socially most productive use.

**10.** So far, our discussion has been concerned with only nationalist commercial policy. In a setting of regional systems of trade, however, the developmental effects of commercial policy may be more substantial. From the theory of economic integration, it may be argued that the establishment of a customs union could play a vital part in promoting a region's development.

When tariffs are removed among members of a customs union, while an external tariff is retained, the development of the members might be accelerated in the following ways: (1) by increasing the gains from trade, (2) by promoting

[41] Cf. Jacob Viner, *International Trade and Economic Development,* The Clarendon Press, 1953, pp. 45-50; Simon Kuznets, *Economic Change,* W. W. Norton & Co., 1953, pp. 222-225.

technical efficiency in existing industries, (3) by stimulating the creation of new industries, and (4) by improving the region's terms of trade.

The analytical framework for this reasoning can be summarized diagrammatically.[42] Consider two countries, A and

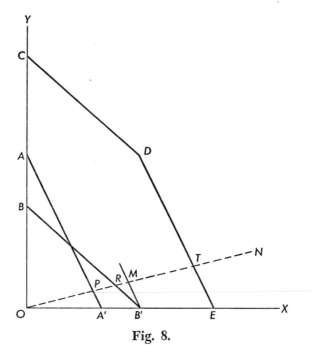

Fig. 8.

B, each capable of producing two commodities, X and Y. Assume a linear production possibility curve for each country as depicted in Fig. 8, where AA' represents the maximum possible combinations of X and Y that can be produced in A,

[42] Cf. H. Makower and G. Morton, "A Contribution Towards a Theory of Customs Unions," *Economic Journal*, March, 1953, pp. 44-45.

with its given factor supply and given techniques of production, and *BB'* represents the maximum possible production combinations of *X* and *Y* in *B*, with its given resources and techniques. Together with its production possibilities, let each country's demand conditions determine its consumption point in isolation as *P* in *A*, and *R* in *B*. For simplicity, *P* and *R* lie on a straight line through the origin, indicating that the consumption pattern is the same in *A* and *B*.

1. If *A* and *B* now form a customs union the total consumption amounts of *X* and *Y* for the two units acting as a single producing area will be greater than the sum of the consumption amounts when *A* and *B* acted in isolation. This can be readily seen by aggregating the production possibilities *AA'* and *BB'*, giving *CDE* in Fig. 8 *(AC = OB, B'E = OA')*. The coordinates of the customs union's consumption point *T* are greater than the sum of the coordinates of *P* and *R*.[43] Thus, when the commodity substitution rates differ in *A* and *B*, and there is not complete specialization in isolation, it is possible to gain from acting as a single producing area and having intra-regional trade: within the customs union there can be more efficient production and hence a higher real income than would be possible if each country remained isolated.

2. This gain may be even greater than that depicted if each country had previously failed to achieve in isolation an optimal allocation of its resources or full employment, but is able to do so through formation of the union. Malallocation

[43] Proof: Draw *B'M* parallel to *A'P*, intersecting *ON* at *M*.
$$OA' = B'E \text{ (by construction).}$$
$$\therefore OP = MT.$$
Total consumption after union = *OT*. Pre-union consumption = *OR* + *MT*. Therefore, post-union consumption is greater than pre-union consumption by the amount *RM*.

or unemployment of resources in $A$ would mean that production and consumption were not at $P$ on the production possibility curve, but to the left of $P$ along $OP$ (assuming the same consumption pattern); similarly, the production and consumption point in $B$ would be not at $R$ but to the left of $R$ along $OR$. To the extent that the consumption points in isolation are to the left of $P$ and $R$, the coordinates of the union's consumption point $T$ would be *pro tanto* superior. If the union creates more internal competition so that marginal firms are forced to improve their methods of production, and resources are reallocated from less efficient to more efficient firms, then economic integration will improve the technical efficiency of existing industries.

3. If now, in addition, the union imposes a protective tariff on imports from non-union countries, then new import-competing industries might be created within the union. If the stimulation of the new industry is not at the expense of a previously existing industry, but comes from an increase in domestic saving or new foreign investment, it will mean an outward shift in the production possibility curve. Thus, if $Y$ is $B$'s import commodity, and a new industry producing $Y$ is established in $B$, the production possibility curve of $B$ will shift out along the $Y$ axis.

4. Finally, the outside tariff might be used to improve the region's commodity terms of trade. Acting in combination, $A$ and $B$ will have stronger bargaining power than if they acted as separate tariff areas, and the region may be able to use this power to raise its own duties on trade with the outside world or to induce outsiders to reduce their duties on their trade with the area. This bargaining power will be more effective in improving the terms of trade the more elastic is the region's reciprocal demand for outside products, and the less elastic is the reciprocal demand of the outside world for

the region's exports. The formation of a customs union might also turn the terms of trade in favor of the union if the intra-union trade is sufficiently large and of such a composition that it reduces the demand within the union for outside imports or reduces the outside supply of the union's exports.

Although the foregoing considerations indicate that the establishment of a customs union might raise the level of development of the region, these theoretical possibilities may not be so significant in practice. Regarding the first possibility of an improved international division of labor, we must note that, unlike the initial situation assumed for Fig. 8, the pre-union situation of prospective members is not one of isolation but, on the contrary, involves high dependence on foreign trade. The formation of a customs union will therefore not only create trade among the members but may also cause some of the existing trade between the members and nonmembers to be replaced by trade within the union. When the liberalization of regional trade has this "trade-diverting effect,"[44] the international division of labor will be worsened to the extent that the outside source of supply is actually a low-cost source and its product becomes higher priced within the union because of the outside duty. The consequence is an uneconomic diversion of output from the low-cost outside source to the high-cost source within the union. World output is reduced, and real income is lowered.

In contrast, if in facilitating trade among members, the union replaces high-cost domestic production by low-cost production from another member, then the effect is one of "trade creation." This constitutes an economic shift of resources into more efficient production.

[44] Jacob Viner, *The Customs Union Issue,* Carnegie Endowment for International Peace, 1950, pp. 48-52; James E. Meade, *The Theory of Customs Unions,* North-Holland Publishing Co., 1955, chap. II.

The expansion of trade within the union, therefore, will not necessarily increase the gains from trade—unless the expanded regional trade is solely from trade creation. Whether trade creation or trade diversion is likely to dominate depends on the pre-union level of tariff rates among the members, the level of post-union external tariff compared with the pre-union tariff level, the elasticities of demand for the imports on which duties are reduced, and the elasticities of supply of exports from the members and foreign sources.[45] Trade creation is more likely to result when: the higher are each member's pre-union duties on the others' products; the more the members are initially similar in the products they produce but different in the pattern of relative prices at which they produce them; the lower is the "average" tariff level on outside imports as compared with the pre-union tariff level; and the less competitive are the products of the members with outside imports. Further, the sort of countries likely to gain more through forming a customs union are those doing a high proportion of their foreign trade with their union partners, and making a high proportion of their total expenditure on domestic trade.[46] Such considerations would indicate that

[45] For a detailed analysis of these considerations, see Meade, *Trade and Welfare, op. cit.*, pp. 527-529; Bela Balassa, *The Theory of Economic Integration*, Richard D. Irwin, Inc., 1961, pp. 25-33.

[46] When the union is formed, the tariff is taken off imports from the country's union partner, and the relative price between these imports and domestic goods is brought into conformity with the real rates of transformation. This tends to raise real income. On the other hand, the relative price between imports from the union partner and imports from the outside world are moved away from equality with real rates of transformation. This tends to reduce real income. Therefore, given a country's volume of international trade, a customs union is on balance more likely to raise real income the higher is the proportion of trade with the country's union partner and the lower the proportion with the outside world. Further, the union is more likely to raise real income the lower is the total volume of foreign trade; for the lower is foreign trade,

when a customs union is composed of a small number of poor countries the possible gains from new trade are likely to be less than they would be in a union composed of "sizeable countries which practice substantial protection of substantially similar industries."[47]

The second possible contribution of a customs union to development—an increase in the productive efficiency of existing industries—may have considerable appeal through the prospect of realizing economies of scale in the wider regional market. But this assumes that the optimum-sized plants are necessarily of a large size, and that the extent of the individual member's market is too small to sustain the large size plant. In many industries, however, technical economies can be exhausted by firms of only moderate size, and even relatively small and poor countries can have a number of firms of the minimum efficient size.[48] This is especially true for light industry in which fixed investment is only a small part of

the lower must be purchases from the outside countries relative to purchases of domestic commodities. R. G. Lipsey, "The Theory of Customs Unions: A General Survey," *Economic Journal*, September, 1960, pp. 507-509.

[47] Viner, *The Customs Union Issue, op. cit.*, p. 135.

[48] But see T. Scitovsky, "Economies of Scale, Competition and European Integration," *American Economic Review*, March, 1956, pp. 71 ff. Scitovsky points out that an economy that is large enough to provide adequate domestic market outlets for the output of at least one optimum-sized plant in all industries producing final goods may still be sub-optimal if some of these plants need equipment, servicing, or other intermediate products, but provide too small a market outlet for some of these. The fact of industrial interdependence therefore makes the scale of output necessary for the full exploitation of economies of scale very much larger than might appear at first thought.

An analysis of the relationships between size of markets, scale of firms and efficiency is also provided in E. A. G. Robinson, ed., *Economic Consequences of Size of Nations*, St. Martin's Press, 1960, Part VI.

total costs. Moreover, an individual member's market is not likely to be extended very much to the wider area of the union unless there is in the pre-union situation a high degree of rivalry for protected industries. It should also be noted that, regardless of the size of the consumer market, if the supply of productive factors is limited, then an industry that is expanding its output will encounter increasing unit costs as the price for its intensive factor rises. Unless the customs union results in a substantial increase in factor mobility among the members, it will not increase the "scale" of the "national" economy from the standpoint of production conditions, even if it does extend it in terms of the size of the protected market for sales.[49]

Finally, it should be realized that there may be more scope for a reduction in an industry's unit-costs, even without a customs union, through a closer approach to the least-cost combination of factors, and hence a downward shift in the entire cost curve, rather than in a movement along a falling cost curve as output expands. The essential point is that the presently low labor productivity results from other conditions besides a small scale of output—namely, inefficient entrepreneurship, unskilled labor, and lack of capital. A better combination of existing factors, an improvement in the quality of existing factors, and the introduction of cost-reducing innovations may all offer more of an increase in productivity than would result from the production of a larger output for a wider market.

The third possibility—the creation of new industries—may provide the largest potential source of gain from a customs union. The prospect of realizing dynamic gains through new investment is likely to be more significant than any static gain from a reallocation of existing production. In its early

[49] Cf. Viner, *The Customs Union Issue, op. cit.,* p. 47.

stages, the union may have more of an effect through the inducement of direct foreign investment to get behind the tariff wall than by a marked expansion in already established industries or the development of industrial products for export. If, however, the union should subsequently entail ever-greater economic integration and coordination of economic, financial, and social policy, then sheltered and export industries might also be more readily created. Centralization of borrowing powers, for example, may improve the prospect for borrowing foreign capital. Common institutional arrangements within the union may also have the important effect of facilitating a regional development program which avoids the wastes of "watertight" compartments of industrialization and the uneconomic multiplication of new industries which might otherwise result from independent industrialization programming by each country.

The last possibility—an improvement in the region's commodity terms of trade—rests on the presumption that the demand by members of the union for imports from outside countries will be reduced, or that the supply of exports from the union will be reduced, or that the bargaining power of the members will be increased. But this depends on whether the poor countries, even within a customs union, could exercise sufficient monopolistic or monopsonistic power to influence their terms of trade. Unless the members of the union are the chief suppliers on the world market or constitute a large part of the world market for their imports, the effects on the terms of trade will be negligible.

**11.** The general conclusion that emerges from the foregoing discussion is that the power of commercial policy to accelerate the development of poor countries is likely to be exaggerated. The specific arguments for protection must be highly qualified, their costs not underestimated, and the advantages of alternative policies not ignored. Some of the objectives sought by a positive commercial policy may be better realized in the context of a customs union, but the practical effects are still unlikely to be as influential as the proponents of a customs union claim.

Of far greater importance to a poor country than the control of its foreign trade is the fundamental problem of how to achieve a more extensive "carry-over" from its export sector to other sectors of the domestic economy. Most poor countries have been able to attain a secular increase in their exports, but this has not succeeded in transmitting development. Unlike the situation in some other countries, the growth in the export sector of a poor country has not propelled the rest of the economy forwards. Instead of limiting our attention to the narrow issue of commercial policy, we should now proceed to examine the broader problem of whether and by what means development can emerge from trade.

# 7  *Development Through Trade*

1.  Dominating all the issues discussed in the preceding chapters is the ultimate question of whether there is a conflict between the gains from trade and the gains from growth. Can foreign trade have a propulsive role in the development of a country? Or, on the contrary, are the dictates of international trade incompatible with the requirements for accelerated development? To the extent that classical and neoclassical economists offered a judgment on this problem, they held that foreign trade could make an impressive contribution to a country's development. Trade was considered to be not simply a device for achieving productive efficiency; it was also an "engine of growth."[1]

There have, however, always been dissenters from this optimistic view—as varied as List, Lenin, and Manoilesco.

[1] D. H. Robertson, "The Future of International Trade," reprinted in American Economic Association, *Readings in the Theory of International Trade*, Blakiston Co., 1949, p. 501.

With the present concern for poor countries, the critics are
now more numerous, and their arguments are far more challenging.[2] At the theoretical level it is frequently contended
that the conclusions from the static equilibrium analysis of
traditional trade theory are irrelevant for interpreting the
problems of development which are inherently dynamic. And
in the historical context, it is argued that international trade
has actually operated as a mechanism of international inequality—widening the gap in the levels of living between
rich and poor countries. The policy implications of these
theoretical and historical arguments are that, even if there
is some cost in sacrificing the gains from international specialization, the poor countries will still realize a net gain by way
of inducing a higher rate of development if they followed
policies of import replacement and deliberate industrialization. It is maintained that, instead of waiting for the transmission of development through trade, the poor countries
would be better off if they directed their own development
towards an expansion of output for their domestic markets.
Just as the theory of the "big push" for a domestic economy
minimizes the importance of fulfilling marginal conditions in
favor of achieving a series of big discontinuous "jumps,"[3] so

[2] Outstanding among these critics are Hans Singer, Raúl Prebisch,
and Gunnar Myrdal. There are, of course, differences of emphasis in
their various arguments. See, H. W. Singer, "The Distribution of Gains
between Investing and Borrowing Countries," *American Economic
Review, Papers and Proceedings,* May, 1950, pp. 473-485; United
Nations, Economic Commission for Latin America, *The Economic Development of Latin America and Its Problems,* New York, 1950, *passim;* Gunnar Myrdal, *Rich Lands and Poor,* Harper & Brothers, 1957,
*passim.*

[3] P. N. Rosenstein-Rodan, "Notes on the Theory of the 'Big Push',"
H. S. Ellis, ed., *Economic Development for Latin America,* St. Martin's
Press, 1961, pp. 57-73; Benjamin Higgins, *Economic Development,*
W. W. Norton & Co., 1959, pp. 384-396.

too is it claimed, in terms of the international economy, that the gains from trade are of only secondary significance compared with the achievement of the gains from growth.

Neither the traditional case for development through trade nor the rival interpretation, however, has been presented in a systematic manner. In this chapter we shall therefore sort out the basic arguments and attempt to clarify the fundamental issues of disagreement. We shall first restate the classical position, appraise the opposing view that international trade has inhibited the development of poor countries, and then suggest alternative reasons why—in spite of their expansion in exports and increased capacity to import—the poor countries have not been able to realize a more significant "carry-over" from external trade to internal development.

**2.**   The problem of the gains from trade versus the gains from growth can be stated as follows. When a country specializes according to its comparative advantage and trades at the international exchange ratio, it gains an increase in real income. As noted in Chapter 2, this gain is tantamount to an outward shift in the country's production frontier, even if the economy operates under the constraints of fixed amounts of resources and unchanged techniques of production. But there still remains the question of whether some other pattern of resource allocation, different from that governed by comparative advantage, might not lead to an even greater outward shift in the production frontier over time. Although the resource allocation associated with trade might conform to requirements for production efficiency in a single period, it is possible that another initial allocation would conform more closely to the multiperiod, not merely single-period, requirements for production efficiency. In other words, there may be a domestic misallocation of resources, from the standpoint of maximizing output over time, even though there is optimal allocation from the standpoint of achieving the gains from trade in each single period.[4]

Such a possible conflict between the gains from trade and the gains from growth was not envisaged in traditional trade theory. Although the dynamic aspects of trade were not central in classical and neoclassical thought, there was nonetheless some recognition, particularly in classical theory, of the dynamic and growth-transmitting aspect of trade above and beyond the static gains from international specialization.[5] In this interpretation, the gains from trade were entirely consistent with the gains from growth; indeed, the latter could be expected to increase *pari passu* with the extension of foreign trade.

John Stuart Mill was especially definite on this. Trade, according to comparative advantage, results in a "more efficient employment of the productive forces of the world," and this may be considered the "direct economical advantage of foreign trade. But," emphasizes Mill, "there are, besides, indirect

[4] This argument simply extends to an open economy the analogous problem of defining an efficient program of capital accumulation for a closed economy. It has been demonstrated that perpetual one-period efficiency can be inefficient over longer periods. The multiperiod requirements for achieving the maximum production frontier in a closed economy are discussed in R. Dorfman, P. A. Samuelson, R. M. Solow, *Linear Programming and Economic Analysis,* McGraw-Hill Book Co., 1958, chap. 12.

[5] Several references of this nature can be cited: in particular, David Ricardo, *Principles of Political Economy and Taxation,* London, 1817, chap. VII; J. S. Mill, *Principles of Political Economy,* London, 1848, Book I, chap. X, section 1; Book III, chap. XVII, section 5; Book IV, chap. II, section 1; Alfred Marshall, "Memorandum on the Fiscal Policy of International Trade," *Official Papers,* Macmillan & Co., 1926; Marshall, *Money, Credit, and Commerce,* Macmillan & Co., 1923, appendix J, sections 8, 10; F. W. Taussig, *Some Aspects of the Tariff Question,* Harvard University Press, 1915, chap. III.

effects, which must be counted as benefits of a high order."
One of the most significant "indirect" dynamic benefits, according to Mill, is "the tendency of every extension of the
market to improve the processes of production. A country
which produces for a larger market than its own, can introduce a more extended division of labour, can make greater
use of machinery, and is more likely to make inventions and
improvements in the processes of production." Another important consideration, "principally applicable to an early
stage of industrial advancement," is that "a people may be
in a quiescent, indolent, uncultivated state, with all their
tastes either fully satisfied or entirely undeveloped, and they
may fail to put forth the whole of their productive energies
for want of any sufficient object of desire. The opening of a
foreign trade, by making them acquainted with new objects,
or tempting them by the easier acquisition of things which
they had not previously thought attainable, sometimes works
a sort of industrial revolution in a country whose resources
were previously undeveloped for want of energy and ambition in the people: inducing those who were satisfied with
scanty comforts and little work, to work harder for the grati-
fication of their new tastes, and even to save, and accumulate
capital, for the still more complete satisfaction of those tastes
at a future time."[6]
Mill also showed his awareness of the special conditions in
poor countries by observing that trade benefits the less developed country through "the introduction of foreign arts,
which raise the returns derivable from additional capital to
a rate corresponding to the low strength of the desire of accumulation; and the importation of foreign capital which
renders the increase of production no longer exclusively de-

[6] Mill, *op. cit.*, vol. II, Book III, chap. XVII, section 5.

pendent on the thrift or providence of the inhabitants themselves, while it places before them a stimulating example,
and by instilling new ideas and breaking the chain of habit,
if not by improving the actual condition of the population,
tends to create in them new wants, increased ambition, and
greater thought for the future."[7]

Considering the classical economists more generally, Hla
Myint has distinguished three different theories of international trade in classical thought: the "vent-for-surplus"
theory, the static comparative costs theory, and a dynamic
"productivity" theory.[8] The "productivity" theory links development to international trade by interpreting trade as a
dynamic force which, by widening the extent of the market
and the scope of the division of labor, permits a greater use
of machinery, stimulates innovations, overcomes technical in-
divisibilities, raises the productivity of labor, and generally
enables the trading country to enjoy increasing returns and
economic development.[9] These gains correspond to Mill's
"indirect effects, which must be counted as benefits of a
high order."

This conception of the impact of trade emphasizes the supply side of the development process—the opportunity that
trade gives a poor country to remove domestic shortages and

[7] Mill, *op. cit.*, vol. I, Book I, chap. XIII, section 1.

[8] Hla Myint, "The 'Classical Theory' of International Trade and the
Underdeveloped Countries," *Economic Journal*, June, 1958, pp. 317-
337. The emphasis on the "vent-for-surplus" theory may be overdone,
for as Professor Haberler has observed, the vent-for-surplus (if it is not
part and parcel of the productivity theory) may be interpreted as
simply an extreme case of differences in comparative costs—a country
exporting commodities for which it has no domestic use. If, however,
this extreme situation exists, it does make trade appear doubly productive and desirable. Gottfried Haberler, *International Trade and
Economic Development*, National Bank of Egypt, 1959, p. 9, n. 1.

[9] Myint, *op. cit.*, pp. 318-319.

to overcome the diseconomies of the small size of its domestic market. Of major benefit is the opportunity that trade offers for the exchange of goods with less growth potential for goods with more growth potential, thereby quickening the progress that results from a given effort on the savings side.[10] An obvious example is the opportunity to import capital goods and materials required for development purposes. Perhaps of even more value than the direct importation of material goods is the fundamental "educative effect" of trade. A deficiency of knowledge is a more pervasive handicap to development than is the scarcity of any other factor. Contact with more advanced economies provides an expeditious way of overcoming this deficiency. The importation of technical know-how and skills is an indispensable source of technological progress, and the importation of ideas in general is a potent stimulus to development. Not only is this vital for economic change in itself, but also for political and socio-cultural advances which may be the necessary preconditions of economic progress. By providing the opportunity to learn from the achievements and failures of the more advanced countries, and by facilitating selective borrowing and adaptation, foreign trade can help considerably in speeding up a poor country's development. As Mill emphasized, "It is hardly possible to overrate the value in the present low state of human improvement, of placing human beings in contact with persons dissimilar to themselves, and with modes of thought and action unlike those with which they are familiar . . . Such communication has always been and is peculiarly in the present age, one of the primary sources of progress."[11]

[10] J. R. Hicks, *Essays in World Economics*, Oxford University Press, 1959, p. 132.

[11] Mill, *op. cit.*, vol. II, Book III, chap. XVII, section 5.

Classical economists also noted the effects of trade on the domestic factor supply, especially on capital accumulation. The capacity to save increases as real income rises through the more efficient resource allocation associated with international trade. And the stimulus to investment is strengthened by the realization of increasing returns in the wider markets that overseas trade provides. Further, by allowing economies of large-scale production, the access to foreign markets makes it profitable to adopt more advanced techniques of production which require more capital; the opportunities for the productive investment of capital are then greater than they would be if the market were limited only to the small size of the home market.[12]

For these several reasons, the traditional conclusion has been that international trade stimulates a country's development. Above and beyond the static gains that result from the more efficient resource allocation with given production functions, international trade also transforms existing production functions and induces outward shifts in the production frontier. The dynamic benefits of trade can be summarized as meaning, in analytical terms, that a movement along the production frontier in accordance with the pre-existing comparative cost situation will tend to push up and out the production frontier.[13] Thus, when they are properly interpreted in their dynamic sense, the gains from trade do not result simply from a once-over change in resource allocation, but

[12] Cf. Hicks, *op. cit.*, pp. 183-185.

[13] Haberler, *op. cit.*, p. 14. Haberler emphasizes in particular four ways in which trade bestows dynamic benefits upon a developing country: the provision of the material means of development in the form of capital goods, machinery and raw and semifinished materials; access to technological knowledge, skills, managerial talents and entrepreneurship; the receipt of capital through international investment; and the stimulating influence of competition (pp. 10-15).

are continually merging with the gains from growth. And if trade increases the capacity for development, then the larger the volume of trade the greater should be the potential for development.

**3.** The foregoing analysis, however, indicates only what could be or what ought to be—not necessarily what has been or is. Indeed, the historical experience of numerous poor countries reveals considerable growth in their foreign trade, but only a slow rate of domestic development. In contrast with what would be expected from classical analysis, the practical question therefore now arises why external trade has induced comparatively little internal development in poor countries.

True, the optimism of the classicists has been vindicated in many cases: international trade did have a propulsive role in the development of a number of countries that are now among the richest in the world. In the case of Britain, development was fostered by the export trade in woolen manufacture and cotton textiles; for Sweden, it was the timber trade; for Denmark, dairy produce; Canada, wheat; Australia, wheat and wool; Switzerland, lace-making and clock-making; Japan, silk. In many historical cases of successful development the importance of international trade is clearly confirmed—and not only for countries that exported industrial products, but also for primary product exporters. At the same time, however, that some countries which were poor a century ago have developed through foreign trade, other countries have still remained poor until the present day, notwithstanding an expansion in their foreign trade.

It is apparent that after a poor country became part of the international economy, its production did increase, but mainly in the direction of production for export. For the poor countries, international trade has frequently been much cheaper and easier than internal trade, and their devotion to international specialization has often been much easier and earlier than specialization among regions within their own countries.[14] A marked secular expansion in exports from the poor countries has consequently been the outstanding result of their integration into world markets. As they entered the international economy, their production for export grew, frequently at an increasing rate and generally at a rate greater than population growth. The variety of exports also became more extensive as more revenue crops were produced and new commodities were established.

On the demand side, this expansion in exports of foodstuffs and raw materials was induced by the growth of richer countries. Their demand for imports of primary products increased as their industrial output rose, their population increased, real income grew, and consumption standards changed. While their demand for primary products rose, the richer countries followed their own comparative advantages in industry and allowed the specialization in primary production to occur overseas.

On the supply side, the movement of resources within the country and the increase in factor supplies also raised the output of exports. External contacts caused a shift of the resources of land and labor away from subsistence production into the production of revenue crops for exchange. In part, there may initially have been some compulsion to earn cash income when the government imposed direct taxes. The movement in this direction persisted, however, because of the desire to improve standards of living and to consume commodities which the subsistence sector did not produce.

[14] Cf. K. E. Berrill, "International Trade and the Rate of Economic Growth," *Economic History Review,* April, 1960, p. 352.

As the imports of manufactured goods increased, another tendency, although of less significance, was the displacement of handicraft workers, and their movement into the export sector. The internal movement of resources has thus been directed towards export production.

Over the longer run, the main contribution to an expansion of exports has come from an increase in factor supplies and technological progress. Owing to the transference of public health measures from the rich countries, the death rate has fallen, and in the absence of a commensurate fall in the birth rate, the population and labor force have grown rapidly. The increasing demand for primary products has also pushed out the extensive margin of land cultivation. For some of these products, it has been relatively easy to duplicate simple techniques of production in the extension of cultivation. For other products, an inflow of capital has come from overseas and has concentrated directly on the development of primary products for export, or else has gone into public overhead capital to facilitate the expansion of exports. Productivity also increased when the direct foreign investment brought with it foreign enterprises that operated under efficient management and with advanced production techniques. To provide an adequate supply of plantation or estate labor, a considerable immigration of labor also occurred in some countries.

These changes in factor supplies may be summarized as having been export-biased. For most poor countries, we may also infer that, because of the nature of their export products, the income elasticity of demand for imports has been greater than for their exportables, and the income effect has been export-biased. Thus, the effects on the production side and consumption side have been on balance export-biased. Even for those cases in which, on the consumption side, the effect may have been import-biased, the net effect is still likely to have been export-biased, insofar as the export-bias in production has probably been sufficiently greater than the import-bias in consumption. Expansion in production has been proportionately greater in the direction of exportables, and this has not been neutralized or reversed on the consumption side.

Nonetheless, despite this increase in exports, the development process has not caught hold in many poor countries. We return to the fundamental question—why has this growth in the export sector not carried over to other sectors and propelled the rest of the economy forwards?

**4.** Critics of the traditional view that trade will transmit development answer this question at two levels—first, by denying the relevance of the conclusions of traditional trade theory, and, secondly, by contending that historically the very forces of international trade have impeded the development of poor countries.

As for the criticisms at the theoretical level, we have already attempted in Chapter 2 to counter the claim that the comparative cost doctrine is irrelevant for problems of economic change. We have seen that it is a relatively simple exercise to incorporate different types of factor growth, technological progress, and changes in the structure of demand into the classical theory of comparative advantage. Although we have done this with the method of comparative statics, short of an explicitly full dynamic theory, this has still carried us a considerable way in interpreting changes in the comparative cost structure. By no means must the conclusions derived from the theory of comparative advantage be limited to a "cross-section" view and a given once-for-all set of conditions; the comparative cost doctrine still has validity among countries undergoing differential rates of development.

Another criticism is directed against the "factor-price equalization theorem" derived from neoclassical theory. This theorem states that, under certain conditions, free international trade is a perfect substitute for complete international mobility of factors and is sufficient to equalize, in the trading countries, not only the prices of products, but also the prices of factors.[15] Against this proposition, however, it is argued that in reality the international distribution of income has become more unequal. And some, like Myrdal, would contrapose against the factor-price equalization theorem a theory of "cumulative causation" or a "cumulative process away from equilibrium in factor proportions and factor prices, engendered by international trade."[16]

This criticism is, however, highly overdrawn. At most, it applies only to the special theorem of complete factor-price equalization—not, as Myrdal implies, to traditional trade theory in general. Proponents of classical theory have never claimed that international trade will actually equalize real wages or real per capita income levels among the trading countries. Far short of this, the contention of classical theory is simply that the real income of each country will be higher with trade than without trade.

Even if the criticism is levied at only the special factor-price equalization theorem, it is still excessive. For it attributes much more importance to the theorem than did its expositors, who recognized its highly restrictive assumptions and hence never maintained that equalization will actually

[15] P. A. Samuelson, "International Trade and the Equalization of Factor Prices," *Economic Journal*, June, 1948, pp. 163-184.

[16] Gunnar Myrdal, *An International Economy*, Harper & Brothers, 1956, p. 225; Myrdal, *Rich Lands and Poor, op. cit.*, chap. 11.

hold or that the theorem is a valid empirical generalization.[17]

The expositors of the factor-price equalization theorem were careful to indicate the limits of the theorem's applicability by emphasizing its dependence on a very special set of assumptions—namely, the existence of perfect competition in all markets, constant returns to scale in the production of each commodity, identical production functions in all countries, and incomplete specialization in all countries (each commodity is produced in all countries). It need not then come with any surprise that factor returns have failed to reach equality between rich and poor countries when factor endowments have been so different that complete specialization has occurred, or economies of scale have led to complete specialization, or production functions have been dissimilar in different countries because of differences in technical knowledge and in the quality of factors, or impediments to trade have existed—when, in short, the restrictive conditions of the theorem have been so clearly violated in reality.

Moreover, we should distinguish between factor-price equalization as inferred from the static model and the inequalities in factor prices which have actually resulted from the historical operation of dynamic forces and changes in the world economy. Only by confusing the static and dynamic problems can it be argued that international trade, instead of equalizing factor prices, has increased the differences. For, in the dynamic setting, trade has been but one of many variables affecting factor prices; it is, therefore, illegitimate to single it out from other dynamic changes as having been the cause of increased inequalities.

[17] P. A. Samuelson, "International Factor-Price Equalization Once Again," *Economic Journal,* June, 1949, p. 182; James E. Meade, *Trade and Welfare,* Oxford University Press, 1955, pp. 332-333. For a review of various statements of the theorem, together with many bibliographical references, see Richard E. Caves, *Trade and Economic Structure,* Harvard University Press, 1960, pp. 76-92.

Finally, the failure to have even a tendency towards factor price equality, let alone full equality, does not mean that measures which bring the economy closer to a fulfillment of the assumptions underlying the theorem might not be effective in diminishing the inequalities, or that trade might not still contribute to a poor country's development. Only by misinterpreting the factor-price equalization theorem, and ignoring all the other dynamic benefits of trade, can the absence of equal factor prices be construed as indicating that trade makes no contribution to development.

5. We may now examine whether historical experience shows that international trade has operated to the detriment of the poor country's development. Unlike the Marxists or others who concentrate on the unfavorable effects of imperialism or colonialism, the modern group of critics does not base its historical critique on any notion of "deliberate exploitation" by the advanced countries. Instead, the emphasis is simply on the free play of international market forces. As argued by Myrdal, "market forces will tend cumulatively to accentuate international inequalities," and "a quite normal result of unhampered trade between two countries, of which one is industrial and the other underdeveloped, is the initiation of a cumulative process towards the impoverishment and stagnation of the latter."[18]

There appear to be three main strands in the argument supporting this conclusion. It is alleged that development has been retarded by first, the unfavorable effects of international factor movements; second, the international operation of the "demonstration effect"; and third, a secular deterioration in the terms of trade. Before offering an alternative explanation of why the poor countries have not succeeded in deriving a

[18] Myrdal, *An International Economy, op. cit.*, pp. 55, 95.

higher rate of development from their foreign trade, we should first appraise this historical interpretation.

The effects of international factor movements, it is claimed,[19] have been adverse in creating a highly unbalanced structure of production. It is maintained that the inflow of foreign capital has developed only the country's natural resources for export, to the neglect of production in the domestic sector. Foreign enterprises have transformed the export sector into the most advanced part of the economy, but this imported western capitalism has not penetrated very far into the indigenous economy. Foreign investments, it is said, have become to a high degree economic enclaves, and even when the enclaves have been large, as in mining or the plantation system, they have seldom been integrated into the local economy, but have remained attached to the interests of a metropolitan state. The result has simply been the creation of a "dual economy" in which production is export-biased, and the export sector remains an island of development surrounded by a backward low-productivity sector.

One version of the dualistic character of poor countries emphasizes the "factor proportions problem" or the "technological dualism" associated with the differences in factor endownment and techniques of production in the advanced "industrial" sector and the backward "pre-industrial" sector.[20]

[19] See, among other sources, *Ibid.*, pp. 27-29, 57-59, chap. 5; Jonathan V. Levin, *The Export Economies*, Harvard University Press, 1960, pp. 4-10, 201-202.

[20] For a detailed analysis of this two-sector model, see R. S. Eckaus, "The Factor Proportions Problem in Underdeveloped Areas," *American Economic Review*, September, 1955, pp. 539-565; Higgins, *op. cit.*, pp. 325-333; H. Leibenstein, "Technical Progress, the Production Function and Dualism," *Banca Nazionale del Lavoro Quarterly Review*, December, 1960, pp. 3-18; International Labour Office, *Employment Objectives in Economic Development*, Geneva, 1961, pp. 27-32.

Features of "dualism" are also stressed in Lewis' model of a high-

The advanced sector is composed of plantation or other large-scale commercial agriculture, mines, oilfields or refineries which produce for export, and large-scale manufacturing, while the backward rural sector is dominated by peasant agriculture, handicrafts, and small-scale industry producing for a local demand. Methods of production in the advanced sector are capital-intensive, and technical coefficients are relatively fixed, whereas in the backward sector production is labor-intensive and the factors of production may be combined in variable proportions. It is contended that the result of this dualism has been that capital, especially foreign capital, flowed into the advanced sector to produce mineral and agricultural products for export markets, but the rate of investment in this sector and labor employment opportunities in the capital-intensive activities did not keep pace with population growth. For lack of alternative employment opportunities, the increasing population therefore had to seek employment in the traditional, variable-coefficient sector. But after a point all available land was cultivated by labor-intensive techniques, and with continuing population growth, disguised unemployment became inevitable in the rural sector. Furthermore, whatever technological progress occurred was biased towards the capital-intensive, fixed-coefficient sector, and the introduction of labor-saving devices

wage capitalist sector and a low-wage noncapitalist sector: W. A. Lewis, "Economic Development with Unlimited Supplies of Labour," *Manchester School of Economic and Social Studies*, May, 1954, pp. 139-191; "Unlimited Labour: Further Notes," *Ibid.*, January, 1958, pp. 1-32.

A sociological interpretation is presented by J. H. Boeke, *Economics and Economic Policy of Dual Societies*, Institute of Pacific Relations, 1953. For a contradiction of Boeke's thesis, see B. Higgins, "The 'Dualistic Theory' of Underdeveloped Areas," *Economic Development and Cultural Change*, January, 1956, pp. 99-115.

diminished still further the capacity of the advanced sector to absorb the population growth. Under such conditions of technological dualism, an expansion in exports may have induced investment and stimulated technological progress in the advanced sector, but it was ineffectual in removing the disguised unemployment or stimulating investment in the backward sector.

It is also argued that foreign-owned plantation and mining enterprises and foreign trading firms have frequently acquired monopsony and monopoly positions.[21] As laborers, the natives have confronted the monopsonistic powers of foreign plantations and mining concerns. As peasant producers, they have faced a small group of exporting and processing firms with monopsonistic powers in buying the native crop. And as consumers, they have had to purchase imported commodities from monopolistic sellers or distributors of these commodities.

Further, it is said that the stimulating income effects of foreign investment have been lost through income leakages abroad.[22] Not only has there been a drain of profits and interest to the capital-exporting countries, but the poor countries have also had to import from the richer countries the capital equipment associated with any investment that has been induced by a growth in exports. The implication is that a given amount of investment in the poor country has generated a much smaller amount of income than the same amount of investment would have generated in a more advanced and less dependent country.

It is also believed that the immigration of unskilled labor

[21] Hla Myint, "An Interpretation of Economic Backwardness," *Oxford Economic Papers*, June, 1954, pp. 154-155; Higgins, *Economic Development, op. cit.*, p. 411.

[22] Singer, *op. cit.*, p. 475.

into poor countries has reinforced the dualistic structure of their economies. In some countries which were at one time sparsely inhabited, the mass immigration of plantation and estate laborers allowed the supply of labor to remain elastic at the conventional low-wage rate. In other countries, labor emigration to richer countries has not been sufficient to exert an upward pressure on wages.

**6.** This critical interpretation of the historical impact of international factor movements has become part of the ideology of economic development in many countries. In contradiction, however, much can be said against such a view of the development-retarding effects of the international migration of capital and labor. The following counterarguments readily suggest themselves.

First, regarding the inflow of capital, we should recognize that since foreign trade has accounted for a large share of governmental revenue, the governments of many poor countries have actually pursued policies designed to attract foreign investment to their export sectors in order to promote their export trade. Moreover, in many instances the chief beneficiaries of foreign investment have been not the foreign investors but groups within the recipient country.[23] For a number of export crops, the production by small holders has also become possible only because of the opportunity to imitate plantation examples and to locate near large-scale enterprises producing the same crop and providing mar-

[23] In the case of British foreign investment in Argentina, for instance, it has been concluded that British investors dominated in the less profitable enterprises, while the really great fortunes accrued to native Argentinos from the appreciation of land values and the profits of pastoral enterprise, commercial agriculture, and share-cropping. H. S. Ferns, *Britain and Argentina in the Nineteenth Century*, Oxford University Press, 1960, pp. 489-490.

keting facilities (as in the case of bananas) or furnishing processing services (sugar cane).

What is most significant, however, is that foreign investment, regardless of its character, has not been competitive with home investment. There is no reason to believe that if there had not been foreign investment, a poor country would have generated more domestic investment; or that, in the absence of foreign entrepreneurs, the supply of domestic entrepreneurs would have been larger. We need not resort to any notion of unbalanced international forces to explain the limited amount of domestic investment and the lack of domestic entrepreneurship: the explanation is apparent in all the domestic obstacles associated with narrow domestic markets and the absence of cooperant factors in sufficient quantity and quality—the very impediments that made foreign capital and technical resources turn away from the domestic towards the export sector.

Much of the criticism is thus misplaced, once it is recognized that the relevant comparison is not between the pattern of resource utilization that actually occurred with international factor movements and some other ideal pattern, but between the actual pattern and the pattern that would have occurred in the absence of the capital and labor inflow. As Nurkse observes, "even 'unbalanced' and unsteady growth through foreign trade was surely much better than no growth at all."[24] If foreign capital and the power of foreign enterprise had resulted in a deliberate diversion of

[24] Ragnar Nurkse, "The Conflict between 'Balanced Growth' and International Specialization," *Lectures on Economic Development,* Faculty of Economics (Istanbul University )and Faculty of Political Sciences (Ankara University), 1958, p. 167. A similar conclusion, based on several historical examples of colonial development, is expressed by W. K. Hancock, *Wealth of Colonies,* Cambridge University Press, 1950, p. 39.

resources from domestic production to the export sector, the arugment would be more serious. The real choice, however, was not so much between using the resources for export production or for domestic production, as between giving employment to the surplus resources in export production or leaving them idle.[25] And over the longer run, the increase in export production was in the form of net additions to output made possible by the utilization of previously idle resources and growth in factor supply, not by a withdrawal from the domestic sector.[26]

Similarly, the complaint about the economic power of foreign enterprises does not demonstrate that development would have been more rapid in the absence of foreign enterprise. All that it implies is that the native's real income might have risen more if he had sold and bought in more competitive markets. But without the impetus from outside, the spread of the exchange economy would have been severely limited in the first place. The power of foreign enterprises can also be exaggerated by overlooking the fact that, on the supply side, the native generally had a reservation price in terms of alternatives between subsistence production, cash cropping, and wage earning.

As for the argument concerning leakages of income abroad, this has simply meant that the secondary round of income effects from an increase in exports would have been larger if there had not been the leakages. The relevant argument, therefore, is for reducing the overseas drain, not for restricting international investment. Without the capital inflow, the

[25] Myint, "The 'Classical Theory' of International Trade and the Underdeveloped Countries," *op. cit.*, p. 11.

[26] Cf. Hla Myint, "The Gains from International Trade and the Backward Countries," *Review of Economic Studies,* vol. XXII (2), No. 58, (1954-55), p. 133.

initial expansion in exports would have been much smaller. Again, the main impetus to the growth of an exchange economy has come from outside, and as the subsistence sector has diminished and the monetary sector has grown, so has the effectiveness of the multiplier process increased. The leakages can also be exaggerated: as exports rose, the demand for local labor and materials increased, sources of taxation expanded, some of the profits were retained and reinvested locally, and by taxation and profit-sharing arrangements the government controlled some of the profit outflow. In many cases, the net payments abroad of interest, dividends, and branch profits have been only minor in relation to the net geographical product of these countries. Consideration should also be given to the fact that the growth in exports from the poor countries was induced by the growth of income in rich countries, and in this sense some of the secondary investment that resulted from an initial increase in demand in the rich countries actually occurred as foreign investment in the poor countries.

Regarding labor immigration, we should note that although it may have tended to keep the wage rate low, it nonetheless did remove the potential barrier of labor scarcity in countries that were sparsely populated, and it did act as a permissive condition for the expansion of exports. Nor should other positive benefits be neglected: in many instances, an entrepreneurial class has come from an originally immigrant group, and expatriate merchants and traders have frequently been responsible for the domestic financing of industries. As for the more general problem of population pressures, one cannot believe that less immigration or any realistic amount of emigration would have been sufficient to remove this problem, in view of the high rates of natural increase due to medical advances. Moreover, the ability to secure additional labor in the export sector at the conventional low wage rate rested ultimately on the low productivity in the subsistence sector.

The over-all contention regarding the effects of factor movement is that the economy of the poor country has suffered a type of structural disequilibrium through its "export bias." But there is some ambiguity as to whether this is meant to imply an absolute overexpansion in the exports of primary products, or merely a relative overexpansion as compared with domestic output.[27] If interpreted in the absolute sense, it implies that the expansion in exports was at the expense of domestic output, and that the economy would have developed more rapidly if exports had been less. Actually, however, there is no convincing evidence that export production was at the expense of home output. And, in view of the comparative cost structure and the essential roles that agriculture and exports must have in the development process, it is difficult to understand how development could have been accelerated by a reduction in exports. If, however, "export bias" implies that the expansion in exports was too rapid relative to growth in domestic output, then it is merely another way of stating the general problem of the lack of carry-over from the export sector to the rest of the economy. "Dualism," or "export bias," or "lack of carry-over," is not an explanation of why the process of derived development has been arrested; instead, it is simply a statement of the problem.

7.   In addition to the adverse consequences of international factor movements, it has also become common to claim that the international operation of the "demonstration effect" has been a handicap for the poor country. It is argued that the

[27] Myint, "The 'Classical Theory' of International Trade and the Underdeveloped Countries," *op. cit.*, p. 335.

demonstration of advanced consumption standards in rich countries has excessively raised the propensity to consume in the poorer countries and has thereby limited capital accumulation. But this effect is easily exaggerated. The emulation of consumption patterns of rich countries could be expected to be strong only for countries which imported secondary products and had a significantly large urban population. Insofar as the imports of some poor countries consisted mainly of foodstuffs and primary products, and the urban component of most populations was small until recently, the demonstration effect was weak.[28]

Moreover, all the relations between rich and poor countries have, in a sense, demonstration effects. Even if one of these effects—that on the propensity to consume—is considered to have been deleterious, the net result of the other effects may have more than offset this. To the extent that the demonstration effect operates in favor of raising the consumption of imported commodities, it operates *pari passu* on the incentives to work and to produce more. Classical economists stressed the incentive side of the demonstration effect, and from the standpoint of accelerating development, this may well outweigh the effect on the consumption side. When the transition to an exchange economy has not been completed, the demonstration effect stimulates more effort to create a marketable surplus of agricultural products, since the ability to purchase new types of consumer goods depends on money income. Extension of the exchange economy entails greater

[28] The "international demonstration effect" was first applied to Western European countries in connection with the postwar dollar shortage problem; see W. F. Stolper, "A Note on Multiplier, Flexible Exchanges and the Dollar Shortage," *Economia Internazionale*, August, 1950, pp. 772-773. Although the demonstration effect may be significant for relations between Western Europe and the United States, it is much weaker for poor countries.

specialization and increased production, and, eventually, additional saving. The general point is that the demonstration effect tends to stimulate the "aspiration to consume" as well as the "propensity to consume" and as long as it affects the aspiration to consume, it may actually lead to greater effort and more production. Indeed, emulation of the urban area by the rural areas has been a contributing element to development in rich countries, and it need not be less favorable simply because it operates internationally.

A demonstration of advanced technological standards has also paralleled the demonstration of advanced consumption standards. In many cases, peasants have been able to adopt a crop introduced and demonstrated by foreign-owned plantations, and in other instances home industries have developed to copy foreign goods. More generally, the demonstration of superior productive techniques in rich countries acts as a constant stimulant to the spread of technology.

8.   The third major criticism of international forces rests on the contention that there has been an international transfer of income from the poor to the rich countries through a secular deterioration in the commodity terms of trade of the poor countries. We have already considered in Chapter 3 the thesis that the commodity terms of trade between industrial and primary producing countries shifted in favor of industrial countries, allegedly because monopolistic elements in their product and factor markets allowed these countries to retain the benefit of their technical progress in the form of rising factor incomes, while in primary producing countries the gains in productivity have been distributed in price reductions. We saw that the statistical foundations for this claim are extremely weak, and that the analytical reasoning is unconvincing. It is difficult to entertain seriously the argument

that the slow pace of development has been due to a worsening in the terms of trade. Even more extreme is the assertion that the case of "immiserizing growth" through a deterioration in the terms of trade has actually occurred. No evidence has been offered that the restrictive conditions necessary for this result have prevailed.

We may also observe that even if the commodity terms of trade had deteriorated, the basic difficulty would have been not the external change in prices, but the failure to have had sufficient internal resource flexibility. If domestic resources were mobile, the distribution of resources would tend to shift from export industries to home-market industries when the commodity terms of trade deteriorate. By inducing shifts in production and in the distribution of resources, a change in the terms of trade would tend to reverse or counteract itself. In other words, changes in the terms of trade are apt to be "washed out" in the long run.[29]

9.    Although we conclude that international market forces did not inhibit development, we are nonetheless left with the question why the classical optimism regarding development through trade has not been vindicated for the poor countries. We must still explain why the gains from trade have not led on to more substantial gains from growth. If the expanding export trade constituted the primary change in the economy, why did it not have more penetrative power and induce more significant secondary changes elsewhere in the domestic economy?

Instead of seeking an answer in the allegedly unfavorable

[29] Ragnar Nurkse, *Patterns of Trade and Development*, Wicksell Lectures, Almquist & Wiksell, 1959, pp. 60-61 (reprinted in *Equilibrium and Growth in the World Economy. Economic Essays by Ragnar Nurkse*, Harvard University Press, 1961, pp. 333-334). Also, C. P. Kindleberger, *The Terms of Trade*, John Wiley & Sons, 1956, pp. 305-308, 311-312.

effects of international trade, we may find a more convincing explanation in the differential effects of different exports, and in the domestic market conditions of the poor country. For, although the initial expansion of the export sector is potentially favorable for development, the actual scale and rapidity with which this stimulus is transmitted to other sectors will depend not only on the rate of export growth, but also on the character of the country's export-base,[30] and on the degree of domestic market imperfections, interpreted in a wide sense. The export stimulus to development will therefore differ among countries, with the export of some countries giving more of a stimulus to development than others.

In the first instance, an increase in export production has a direct effect on the growth of the economy, but in addition there are indirect effects which are extremely important in determining to what extent development can be stimulated through foreign trade. Some of these indirect consequences can be associated with the different forms of the production functions of particular export commodities.[31]

[30] Some essentials of an export-base theory of regional economic development have been discussed by A. F. W. Plumptre, "The Nature of Political and Economic Development in the British Dominions," *Canadian Journal of Economics and Political Science*, November, 1937, pp. 489-507; D. C. North, "Location Theory and Regional Economic Growth," *Journal of Political Economy*, June, 1955, pp. 249-251; C. M. Tiebout, "Exports and Regional Economic Growth," *Journal of Political Economy*, April, 1956, pp. 160-164; North, "Agriculture in Regional Economic Growth," *Journal of Farm Economics*, December, 1959, pp. 943-951.

The "staple approach" to economic history, often applied by Canadian economic historians, also focuses upon the stimulating role that staple exports have in the process of development; see, for example, K. Buckley, "The Role of Staple Industries in Canada's Economic Development," *Journal of Economic History*, 1958, pp. 439-450; R. E. Caves and R. H. Holton, *The Canadian Economy*, Harvard University Press, 1959, pp. 30-47, 141-144, 387.

[31] For discussions of the importance of production functions to eco-

One consequence is that with various factor combinations being used to product different export commodities, the export industries will differ in their income distribution. In broad terms, the relative shares of profits, wages, interest, and rent will vary according to whether the export product comes from mining, plantation agriculture, or peasant farming. We would expect, for instance, from the different types of organization of the tin and rubber industries, that the ratio of profits to wages would be higher for tin than for rubber. And, given the same increase in exports in the two industries, the direct effect of the tin industry on employment and personal income will be smaller than for the rubber industry. When the export commodity is produced by both peasants and plantations, or by both private mines and company mines, the internal distribution of the export income will also differ according to the relative shares of the output produced by each type of organization.

Along with the diverse patterns of domestic distribution of export income, it is also likely that the structure of demand and saving propensities will differ among poor countries. The pattern of consumption will be directed more to home-produced commodities in one economy than in another, in which the distribution of income favors groups with higher propensities to import. The ratio of savings to income, for comparable per capita incomes, may also be higher in one type of economy than another. And the investment which the savings

nomic development, see R. E. Baldwin, "Patterns of Development in Newly Settled Regions," *Manchester School of Economic and Social Studies*, May, 1954, pp. 161-179; Dudley Seers, "An Approach to the Short-Period Analysis of Primary-Producing Economies,"*Oxford Economic Papers*, February, 1959, pp. 6-9; Caves and Holton, *op. cit.*, pp. 41-47; Boris C. Swerling, "Some Interrelationships between Agricultural Trade and Economic Development," *Kyklos*, vol. XIV, No. 3 (1961), pp. 377-379.

make possible may be more productive in one economy than another. To the extent that variations in conditions of demand, and in the supply and utilization of saving, are related to the type of export production, different export industries vary in their influence on the development process.

This emphasis on the nature of the export commodity's production function extends beyond the "factor proportions problem" (discussed in section 5, above). In affecting the distribution of income, the pattern of consumption, and the use of savings, the nature of the production in the export sector has implications other than those of technological dualism. Even the conditions of technological dualism are highly special and do not exist to the same extent in different poor countries. Not all types of exports can be characterized as being produced under capital-intensive and fixed-coefficient conditions; the degree of capital intensity and factor substitutability varies from commodity to commodity. Moreover, even if all the exports of different countries were produced with a high capital-labor ratio and did not provide much employment to labor, other industries that are linked to exports might still differ in capital-intensity and factor substitutability among the various countries.

A significant implication of the "factor proportions problem," however, is that the extent to which modern processing techniques are used in export production is important in determining the strength of the stimulus from exports. The machine processing of raw materials or foodstuffs increases employment and creates income in other activities supporting the export sector, such as the supplying of materials, tools and implements, transportation, and construction. Even more important, the degree to which the various exports are processed is significant in determining the amount of machinery used, the spread of technical knowledge, the development of labor skills available for other types of industry, and the diffusion of organizational and administrative skills. It also increases the scope for innovations in the export sector. Thus, when the processing of primary product exports by modern methods sets in motion a chain of further modern sector requirements and provides external economies, the export sector may, in Rostow's terminology, play a strong role as the leading sector in the take-off into self-sustained growth.[32]

In contrast, even though it may have the highest growth rate in the economy, the export sector will provide only a weak stimulus if its techniques of production are the same as those already in use in other sectors, and if its expansion can occur by a simple widening of production without any change in production functions. The ability to expand export production without introducing new techniques of production has been a feature of some peasant export sectors. In some cases, when the export crop was a traditional crop, the growth in export output was achieved simply by bringing more land under cultivation with the same methods of cultivation used in the subsistence sector. In other instances, when new export crops were introduced, their success as peasant export crops was determined by the fact that they involved simple methods of production that did not differ markedly from the traditional techniques used in subsistence agriculture.[33] When the export expansion of peasant crops merely reproduced existing production conditions on a larger scale, the stimulus to development was less than it would have been if the expansionary process had entailed the intro-

[32] W. W. Rostow, *The Stages of Economic Growth*, Cambridge University Press, 1960, pp. 39, 56.

[33] Cf. Myint, "The Classical Theory of International Trade and the Underdeveloped Countries," *op. cit.*, p. 321.

duction of new skills and more productive recombinations of factors.

The repercussions from exports also differ according to the degree of fluctuation in export proceeds. Disruptions in the flow of foreign exchange receipts make the development process discontinuous; the greater is the degree of instability, the more difficult is it to maintain steady development. The larger is the amplitude of fluctuation, the greater is the effect on employment, real income, capital formation, resource allocation, and the capacity to import.

Fluctuations in retained proceeds from exports may also affect the internal distribution of income, and in different ways for different types of economies. For instance, it may be that in a peasant economy the middlemen have been able to maintain fairly constant rates of profits on the external prices of exports and imports by shifting the burden of cyclical adjustments on to the peasants, while in a mineral or plantation economy profits have borne more of the adjustment.[34] And when the impact of fluctuations in an export industry falls on wages or employment, the effects on labor's income will vary according to whether labor can shift into another export industry, domestic industry, or subsistence farming.

From a consideration of various characteristics of the country's export-base, we may thus infer how the strength of the stimulus from exports will differ among countries. In summary, we would normally expect the stimulus to be stronger under the following conditions: the higher is the growth rate of the export sector; the greater is the direct effect in the export sector on employment and personal income; the less the distribution of export income favors those with a higher

[34] Myint, "The Gains from International Trade and the Backward Countries," *op. cit.*, pp. 132-133; Levin, *op. cit.*, pp. 186-193.

marginal propensity to import; the more productive is the investment resulting from any saving of export income; the more exports expand through a change in production functions, rather than by a simple widening process; and the more stable are retained export receipts.

If we have so far looked to the character of a country's export base for an indication of the strength of the export stimulus to development, we must now look to market conditions within the domestic economy for evidence of how receptive the economy is to the stimulus from exports. For, when intersectoral relationships are many and the response to an expansion in exports is rapid and extensive in scope, then even a weak stimulus can still result in a significant carry-over. In contrast, when there are formidable domestic impediments to a transmission of the gains from exports to other sectors, then even a strong stimulus will have only slight penetrative power.

In connection with these domestic impediments, we can recognize that the pervasiveness of market imperfections has severely limited the carry-over from exports. The economies of poor countries are characterized by factor immobility, price rigidity, restrictive tendencies in both the factor and good markets, ignorance of technological possibilities, limited knowledge of market conditions, and few centers of entrepreneurship. All these imperfections handicap the achievement of intertemporal efficiency in the utilization of resources. Although the monetary sector of the economy has expanded, this does not mean that there is yet a well-articulated price system which promotes specialization and coordinates activities. Though local markets for the sale of surplus products have grown in volume and variety, and there has been a movement of labor into wage employment, the price system certainly does not operate as effectively as in a more advanced economy. The functions of the price system are narrowly constrained in an economy in which markets are local, subsistence production accounts for a substantial proportion of national product, and traditional rules and customary obligations prevail. There are then definite limits to the extent to which the price system can operate as an instrument for development.[35]

Many of these inhibiting factors are a function of sociocultural customs and institutions.[36] While economic change in itself, especially those change-inducing factors introduced through international contacts, may help to transform traditional customs and mores, there is still a need for indigenous forces of sociological and political development. When political and social policies have maintained conditions under which the traditional village system has persisted; when the value structure of the society has placed little emphasis on a concern about the future, or on man's mastery of nature; when even the government of the poor country has remained economically backward in the sense of being unable to formulate and administer economic policies—when all these hin-

[35] Cf. H. A. Innis, "The Penetrative Powers of the Price System," *Canadian Journal of Economics and Political Science*, August, 1938, pp. 299-319. But see, Eric E. Lampard, "The Price System and Economic Change, A Commentary on Theory and History," *Journal of Economic History*, December, 1960, pp. 617-637.

[36] The literature on development has given increasing attention to the cultural, social, and psychological factors which operate to inhibit development. See, for example, J. L. Saide, "The Social Anthropology of Economic Underdevelopment," *Economic Journal*, June, 1960, pp. 294-303; Ralph Linton, "Cultural and Personality Factors Affecting Economic Growth," in B. F. Hoselitz, ed., *The Progress of Underdeveloped Areas*, University of Chicago Press, 1952; "Symposium on Economic Motivations and Incentives in a Traditional and in a Modern Environment," *International Social Science Bulletin*, vol. VI, No. 3, 1954, pp. 369-476 (with bibliography); D. C. McClelland, *The Achieving Society*, D. Van Nostrand Co., 1961.

drances to change have existed within the domestic economy, it is understandable why the stimulus from the export sector has not been sustained.

In terms of Rostow's schema, the failure of the export sector to have been a primary growth sector, setting in motion expansionary forces elsewhere in the economy, may be attributed in large part to the absence of the preconditions necessary for a take-off into self-sustained growth. While their exports rose, many poor countries at the same time had not yet experienced the second stage of growth—a transitional era when the politics, social structure, and values of a traditional society are altered in such ways as to permit regular growth.[37]

No matter how strong is the stimulus from foreign trade, what is essential is that the prior development of the society and its economy should result in a positive and self-reinforcing response to it. If this necessary foundation exists, international trade can then release latent indigenous forces which can exploit, in turn, the stimulus from the export sector and produce further transformative effects throughout the economy. Historical cases of successful development through trade demonstrate that a prior accumulation of economic experience and the establishment of already-existing trades and channels of trade had a strong influence upon the success with which further development was pursued. Unlike this favorable situation, however, the domestic economy of

[37] Rostow, *op. cit.*, chaps. 2-4. Although the economists concerned with economic development, and even the economic historians, have concentrated almost exclusively on the period of the "take-off" and the period of "self-sustaining growth," it is the earlier period of the emergence of the preconditions for development that is still most relevant for many poor countries. An understanding of this period is most important, yet it is the most difficult to explain and remains the least understood.

the poor country has remained fragmented and compart-
mentalized, the transference of resources from less productive
to more productive employment has been restricted, and the
linkage of markets and their subsequent extension have been
handicapped. The secondary round of activities induced by
an increase in exports has thereby been cut short, and the
dynamic gains from trade have not been fully realized.

We thus conclude that the domestically-based obstacles to
development have been of much greater significance than
any external obstacles, and that if the internal handicaps had
been less formidable, the stimuli from foreign trade would
have been more effective in inducing responses favorable to
technical progress, entrepreneurship, and capital accumulation.

**10.** If the penetrative power of foreign trade has been
limited by domestic handicaps, instead of by the nature of
international trade itself, there is a greater likelihood that the
development through trade mechanism may yet be effective
in poor countries, as it has been in many other countries. For
if the obstacles are within the domestic economy, they are
likely to be more amenable to change through suitable policy
measures than would be the case if changes in the structure
of international trade were required.

Mindful of the potential contribution that foreign trade
can make to development, we have submitted that the basic
international trade problem for a poor country is not so much
how to control its trade, but rather how to achieve a more
extensive carry-over from its export trade to its domestic
economy. Many of the policy implications of the foregoing
analysis thus center upon a reduction in the market imperfections. To accomplish this, alternative forms of economic and
social organization are required. If the export sector is to be

able to propel the rest of the economy forwards, domestic policies must concentrate on diminishing the prevalence of semimonopolistic and monopolistic practices, removing restraints on land tenure and land use, widening the capital market, and making credit and marketing facilities more readily available. The economy must also be made more flexible through investment in transportation, communication, education, and manpower training. If the market imperfections are reduced, the development process may then be more readily established on an indigenous base within the society of the poor country.

If market imperfections are eliminated, and the internal economic structure becomes more flexible, the penetrative power of foreign trade can be greater. Modern production techniques can be diffused more widely. New skills can be created and transferred to domestic enterprises. Entrepreneurial activities can also be expanded, since entrepreneurship depends not only on individual abilities and motivations but also on a congenial environment for the individual. And investment can be greater, with a higher rate of plough-back of foreign exchange proceeds into the investment opportunities created by foreign trade. Insofar as this investment is directed to industries related to exports, either in servicing exports or using an import material as an input for home industry, the investment can be more productive than the short-run speculative type of investment that has been only too prevalent.

Against this emphasis on the removal of domestic obstacles as a means of increasing the stimulating effect of exports, it may be argued that while this is an appropriate consideration when the stimulus from exports is strong, it is not relevant when exports do not provide much of a stimulus in the first place. Granted that domestic obstacles may have accounted for the weak carry-over of exports in the past when export markets were expanding, there remains a possibility that now exports may no longer enjoy a strongly rising world demand and may not be a sufficient basis for development. If exports cannot be relied upon to grow sufficiently, then foreign trade will be a weak transmitter of development even if the domestic obstacles are removed. It might be claimed that comparative costs should not be relied upon as an allocative mechanism—that the dictates of comparative advantage may lead only to comparative stagnation if the country's exports face an external demand which has low elasticity with respect to price and income, and the total volume of exports increases at only a slow rate.[38] In this situation, however, it becomes all the more necessary to strengthen the country's export position and follow policies that make the domestic economy as flexible as it can be in order that the response to even a weak external stimulus may be as extensive as possible.

Even if the price elasticity of demand for a primary product export is generally low, it may be high from a single source of supply. If the prices of substitute products rise relatively to the price of the primary product export, the

[38] Nurkse has maintained that the "incremental" comparative advantage of primary producers in their traditional exports is low, and that because of the limitations of export markets, the forces making for the transmission of growth are not as powerful now as in the past. "The Conflict between 'Balanced Growth' and International Specialization," *op. cit.*, pp. 176-177; *Patterns of Trade and Development, op. cit.*, pp. 19-27, 54-55. But see, A. K. Cairncross, "International Trade and Economic Development," *Kyklos*, vol. XIII, No. 4 (1960), pp. 546-550; "International Trade and Economic Development," *Economica*, August, 1961, pp. 242-249. Cairncross questions Nurkse's argument and submits that domestic supply elasticities and domestic policies, rather than world demand conditions, have been the dominating factor in limiting the growth of exports of primary produce.

volume of exports may also increase. It is therefore necessary for the poor country to improve its competitive position in export markets and its cost advantage over substitutes by increasing productivity and restraining internal demand. Since it is highly improbable that all primary products should face unfavorable growth prospects, poor countries must also pursue policies ensuring that they are specializing as much as they can in exports with the highest growth prospects. This requires, in turn, a capacity to reallocate resources. To shift, for example, from the production of a foodstuff export, which faces only a slowly growing demand, to an industrial raw material or a mineral export, which has a more rapidly expanding demand, will entail structural changes and greater mobility of resources.

At the same time, the removal of tariffs and quotas on imports of primary products into industrialized countries would also improve the export prospects of poor countries. So would the avoidance of artificial support of synthetic substitute products. Above all, higher rates of growth in advanced countries will also strengthen export possibilities.

Inasmuch as the short-term fluctuations in export proceeds also affect development, policy measures should be designed to mitigate the volatile movements, especially the substantial falls, in export earnings. Of prime importance is the maintenance of import demand through high and stable levels of employment in industrial countries. But, in addition, national and international action might be taken to achieve greater short-run stability in international commodity markets. Various stabilization techniques are possible: buffer pools, quota systems, long-term contracts, coordinated national stockpiling schemes, and statutory marketing boards. Instead of dealing with individual commodities and attempting to stabilize their prices, an alternative approach is through some form of countercyclical lending. Commodity prices may be left free to fluctuate, so as to avoid interference with long-run adjustments in production, but the domestic impact of falling prices may be offset by having producer countries receive compensatory financial assistance in the form of loans or grants from the surplus consumer countries or international institutions.[39] Through more effective monetary and fiscal measures, the government of the poor country may also restrain inflation and accumulate exchange reserves during the period of rising export proceeds, and then draw on the accumulated reserves during a downswing to maintain imports essential for development.

Beyond the benefits from improvements in the position of their traditional primary exports, the poor countries may be able to take advantage of new export opportunities for manufactured goods. The exportation of cheap labor-intensive manufactured commodities may provide an increasingly important opportunity for transmitting development to some poor countries which have the necessary resources and can gain a comparative advantage by utilizing labor-intensive methods.[40] It may be only through production for export that

[39] For a discussion of the details of various stabilization schemes, and an appraisal of their relative merits, see United Nations, Department of Economic Affairs, *Measures for International Economic Stability*, New York, 1951; P. T. Bauer and F. W. Paish, "The Reduction of Fluctuations in the Incomes of Primary Producers," *Economic Journal*, December, 1952, pp. 750-780; Symposium on "The Quest for a Stabilization Policy in Primary-Producing Countries," *Kyklos*, 1958, pp. 139-265; "Stabilization and Development of Primary-Producing Countries, Symposium II," *Kyklos*, 1959, pp. 269-401; Henry C. Wallich, "Stabilization of Proceeds from Raw Material Exports," H. S. Ellis, ed., *Economic Development for Latin America*, St. Martin's Press, 1961, pp. 342-366.

[40] The desirability of this solution is discussed by Nurkse, *Patterns of Trade and Development*, op. cit., pp. 36-41; W. A. Lewis, "Employment Policy in an Underdeveloped Area," *Social and Economic*

a poor country can overcome the small size of its home market and become efficient in industries that need a wide market in order to realize economies of scale. It is unlikely, however, that capital goods or the products of heavy industry can be successfully exported because they require considerable capital and large-scale methods. It is also difficult for a poor country to compete in the export market for manufactured consumer goods that have exacting requirements of style and quality, or in exports that may confront a protectionist barrier in advanced countries. Yet, there may be considerable opportunity to export consumer goods, particularly textiles and light manufactures, to other less developed countries. This is especially likely if they are members of some form of free trade area or customs union, as discussed in Chapter 6. There may also be substantial markets, in both the advanced and other developing countries, for the exports of some light manufactures, and for processed primary products from materials-oriented industries, which can advantageously locate at the source of the raw materials. In these situations, the export of manufactures may become a direct means of industrialization, in contrast with the export of primary staples, which provides only a basis for inducing industrialization through a gradual process of development.

Thus, in the future for currently poor countries, as in the past for other countries, foreign trade may operate as an engine of growth transmission—provided there are latent indigenous forces of development that can be released through trade. The gains from trade can facilitate development, but

*Studies,* September, 1958, pp. 47-48; *Trends in International Trade: A Report by a Panel of Experts,* GATT, Geneva, October, 1958, p. 80; Hal B. Lary, "Economic Development and the Capacity to Import—National Policies," *Lectures on Economic Development, op. cit.,* pp. 136-138.

they cannot be a substitute for the developmental forces that must necessarily be created within the domestic economy. And these forces cannot be viewed as comprising only the basic economic determinants of development, such as entrepreneurship, technical progress, and capital accumulation. For these proximate determinants are, in turn, related to the indirect noneconomic, but nonetheless highly important, influences of the society's political, social, and institutional organization. The merging of the gains from trade with the gains from growth rests ultimately, therefore, on the efficacy of domestic policy measures in producing sufficient social and political change, as well as economic change, to make the economy more responsive to the stimulus from trade. If this is accomplished, the benefits of international specialization may then be secured—not only for economic efficiency, but also for the urgent challenge of accelerating development.

# Selected Bibliography

The following bibliographical notes provide some guidance to the reader who wants to pursue more extensive reading on the central issues discussed in this book. Although detailed references on specific points have been offered in the numerous footnotes to the text, it may be useful to provide here a broader list of readings. A few of the readings are of a background character, but most supplement the text's discussion of major topics.

1. The extensive literature on the economics of development may best be approached by consulting the following bibliographies: Arthur Hazlewood, *The Economics of 'Under-Developed' Areas, An Annotated Reading List of Books, Articles, and Official Publications,* (Oxford University Press, 1959); Frank N. Trager, "A Selected and Annotated Bibliography on Economic Development, 1953-1957," *Economic Development and Cultural Change,* July, 1958; United Nations Headquarters Library, *Bibliography on Industrialization in Under-Developed Countries,*

## 194 International Trade and Development

(Bibliographical Series No. 6, 1956). Several of the economic development textbooks also contain useful bibliographies.

2. A comprehensive bibliography on international trade is contained in H. S. Ellis and Lloyd Metzler, eds., *Readings in Theory of International Trade*, (Blakiston Co., 1949). A more recent and selective reading list is furnished by Gottfried Haberler, *A Survey of International Trade Theory*, (International Finance Section, Princeton University, second edition, 1961); also by R. E. Caves, *Trade and Economic Structure* (Harvard University Press, 1960).

3. Several excellent expositions of the traditional theory of international trade may be cited. Jacob Viner's *Studies in the Theory of International Trade* (Harper & Brothers, 1937) is unrivalled for its scholarly treatment of the history of doctrine and for its statement of the classical theory of comparative costs and international values. Among the many studies of modern developments in the pure theory of trade, the following deserve special mention: W. W. Leontief, "The Use of Indifference Curves in the Analysis of Foreign Trade," *Quarterly Journal of Economics,* May, 1933 (reprinted in *Readings in Theory of International Trade,* chap. 10); Gottfried Haberler, "Some Problems in the Pure Theory of International Trade," *Economic Journal,* June, 1950; James E. Meade, *A Geometry of International Trade,* (George Allen & Unwin, 1952); Meade, *Trade and Welfare,* (Oxford University Press, 1955); Kelvin Lancaster, "The Heckscher-Ohlin Trade Model: A Geometric Treatment," *Economica,* February, 1957; R. E. Caves, *Trade and Economic Structure,* (Harvard University Press, 1960); R. A. Mundell, "The Pure Theory of International Trade," *American Economic Review,* March, 1960; Jacob Viner, "Relative Abundance of Factors and International Trade," *Indian Economic Journal,* January, 1962.

4. Although there is no single volume that provides a compre-

hensive analysis of the interrelations between trade and development, several writers have considered various aspects of international trade from the viewpoint of poor countries. Some fundamental development problems are interpreted in the context of the international setting by the following: Jacob Viner, *International Trade and Economic Development*, (Free Press, 1952); J. R. Hicks, *Essays in World Economics*, (Oxford University Press, 1959), chap. 8; and C. P. Kindleberger, "Foreign Trade and Economic Growth: Lessons from Britain and France, 1850 to 1913," *Economic History Review*, December, 1961. Analyses of a more formal character are presented by Trygve Haavelmo, *A Study in Theory of Economic Evolution*, (North-Holland Publishing Co., 1954), Part V, and Staffan Burenstam Linder, *An Essay on Trade and Transformation*, (John Wiley & Sons, 1961). An interesting perspective on the relation of classical trade theory to development problems is given by Hla Myint, "The 'Classical Theory' of International Trade and the Underdeveloped Countries," *Economic Journal*, June, 1958. Gottfried Haberler's Cairo lectures on *International Trade and Economic Development*, (National Bank of Egypt, 1959) are highly instructive in bringing the tools of traditional theory to bear upon the problem of the contribution which foreign trade can make to economic development. The most extensive and provocative discussion of the relation of trade to development is to be found in the writings of Ragnar Nurkse: "Some International Aspects of the Problem of Economic Development," *American Economic Review, Papers and Proceedings*, May, 1952; *Problems of Capital Formation in Underdeveloped Countries*, (Basil Blackwell, 1953), chaps. III-VI; "The Conflict between 'Balanced Growth' and International Specialization," in *Lectures on Economic Development*, (Istanbul, 1958); *Patterns of Trade and Development*, Wicksell Lectures, (Stockholm, 1959); "International Trade Theory and Development Policy," H. S. Ellis, ed., *Economic Development for Latin America*, (St. Martin's Press, 1961). The Istanbul lecture and Wicksell Lectures are reprinted in *Equilibrium and Growth in the World Economy, Economic Essays by Ragnar Nurkse,* (Harvard University Press, 1961). A well-balanced appraisal of the arguments in Haberler's Cairo Lectures and Nurkse's Wicksell Lectures is contained in A. K. Cairncross' review article, "International Trade and Economic Development," *Kyklos,* vol. XIII, No. 4 (1960). Cairncross also questions Nurkse's argument in his later article, "International Trade and Economic Development," *Economica,* August, 1961.

5.    Several models have been presented for analyzing the forces affecting the structure of comparative costs and movements in the terms of trade between developing economies. An early model was set forth in J. R. Hicks' "Inaugural Lecture," *Oxford Economic Papers,* June, 1953. Hicks clarifies this model in his *Essays in World Economics,* Note B. The most thorough analysis is contained in Harry G. Johnson's "Economic Expansion and International Trade," *Manchester School of Economic and Social Studies,* May, 1955 [revised and extended as chap. III in his *International Trade and Economic Growth,* (Harvard University Press, 1958)]; also "Economic Development and International Trade," *Pakistan Economic Journal,* December, 1959. A good summary of Johnson's analysis is offered in the review article of Johnson's book by Jagdish Bhagwati, "The Theory of International Trade," *Indian Economic Journal,* July, 1960. A number of other articles relate to Johnson's model, and are helpful in clarifying the effects of a country's development on its pattern of trade and terms of trade. Especially illuminating are W. M. Corden, "Economic Expansion and International Trade: A Geometric Approach," *Oxford Economic Papers,* June, 1956; John Black and Paul Streeten, "La balance Commerciale les termes de l'échange et la croissance économique," *Economie Appliquée,* April-September, 1957 [an English version appears as the Appendix to Paul Streeten's *Economic Integration,* (A. W. Sythoff, 1961)]; Kurt M. Savosnick, "The Box Diagram and the Production Possibility Curve," *Ekonomisk Tidskrift,* September,

1958; Jagdish Bhagwati, "Immiserizing Growth: A Geometrical Note," *Review of Economic Studies,* June, 1958; Bhagwati, "International Trade and Economic Expansion," *American Economic Review,* December, 1958; Bhagwati, "Growth, Terms of Trade and Comparative Advantage," *Economia Internazionale,* August, 1959. An important article showing the effect of factor-endowment changes on trade is by T. M. Rybczynski, "Factor Endowment and Relative Commodity Prices," *Economica,* November, 1955. The relationships between technological progress and comparative costs are sorted out by R. Findlay and H. Grubert, "Factor Intensity, Technological Progress, and the Terms of Trade," *Oxford Economic Papers,* February, 1959; also, Harry G. Johnson, "Effects of Changes in Comparative Costs as Influenced by Technical Change," *Malayan Economic Review,* October, 1961. An interesting analysis of the effects of capital formation on trade is contained in D. M. Bensusan-Butt's "Model of Trade and Accumulation," *American Economic Review,* September, 1954.

On the allegedly adverse secular trend in the terms of trade of underdeveloped countries, the following are especially noteworthy: R. E. Baldwin, "Secular Movements in the Terms of Trade," *American Economic Review, Papers and Proceedings,* May, 1955; P. T. Ellsworth, "The Terms of Trade between Primary Producing and Industrial Countries," *Inter-American Economic Affairs,* Summer, 1956; Theodore Morgan, "The Long-Run Terms of Trade between Agriculture and Manufacturing," *Economic Development and Cultural Change,* October, 1959; Gottfried Haberler, "Terms of Trade and Economic Development," H. S. Ellis, ed., *Economic Development for Latin America,* (St. Martin's Press, 1961); Jagdish Bhagwati, "A Skeptical Note on the Adverse Secular Trend in the Terms of Trade of Underdeveloped Countries," *Pakistan Economic Journal,* December, 1960.

6. The principles of balance of payments analysis set forth in James E. Meade's *Balance of Payments,* (Oxford University

Press, 1951), and Harry G. Johnson's *International Trade and Economic Growth,* (Harvard University Press, 1958), chap. VI, provide a helpful background for understanding the balance of payments problems of developing countries. An excellent discussion of the balance of payments effects of capital formation is presented by Ragnar Nurkse, "The Relation between Home Investment and External Balance in the Light of British Experience, 1945-1955," *Review of Economics and Statistics,* May, 1956 [reprinted in *Equilibrium and Growth in the World Economy,* (Harvard University Press, 1961)]. Also of special interest are the following: H. C. Wallich, "Underdeveloped Countries and the International Monetary Mechanism," *Money, Trade, and Economic Growth. Essays in Honor of J. H. Williams,* (Macmillan & Co., 1951); E. M. Bernstein and I. G. Patel, "Inflation in Relation to Economic Development," *I. M. F. Staff Papers,* November, 1952; Felipe Pazos, "Economic Development and Financial Stability," *Ibid.,* October, 1953; E. M. Bernstein, *et al.,* "Economic Development with Stability," *Ibid.,* February, 1954; Henry J. Bruton, "Productivity, the Trade Balance and the Terms of Trade," *Economia Internazionale,* August, 1955; J. C. Ingram, "Capital Imports and the Balance of Payments," *Southern Economic Journal,* vol. XXII, No. 4, and "Growth in Capacity and Canada's Balance of Payments," *American Economic Review,* March, 1957; K. K. Kurihara, "Economic Development and the Balance of Payments," *Metroeconomica,* March, 1958; W. M. Corden, "The Geometric Representation of Policies to Attain Internal and External Balance," *Review of Economic Studies,* October, 1960.

7.   A broad survey of the role of foreign investment in poor countries is provided by C. Wolf and S. C. Sufrin, *Capital Formation and Foreign Investment in Underdeveloped Areas,* (Syracuse University Press, 1955); an annotated bibliography is also appended. The most rigorous analysis of the benefits and costs of private foreign investment is to be found in Sir Donald

MacDougall's "The Benefits and Costs of Private Investment from Abroad: A Theoretical Approach," *Economic Record,* March, 1960 (reprinted in *Bulletin of the Oxford University Institute of Statistics,* August, 1960). Also highly illuminating are the discussions in H. W. Arndt's "A Suggestion for Simplifying the Theory of International Capital Movements," *Economia Internazionale,* August, 1954, and "Overseas Borrowing—the New Model," *Economic Record,* August, 1957; J. Knapp, "Capital Exports and Growth," *Economic Journal,* September, 1957; T. Balogh and P. P. Streeten, "Domestic versus Foreign Investment," *Bulletin of the Oxford University Institute of Statistics,* August, 1960 (revised as chap. 4 in Streeten's *Economic Integration*); A. K. Cairncross, "The Contribution of Foreign and Domestic Capital to Economic Development," *International Journal of Agrarian Affairs,* April, 1961.

A perceptive analysis of the problem of debt servicing is furnished by G. M. Alter, "The Servicing of Foreign Capital Inflows by Underdeveloped Countries," H. S. Ellis, ed., *Economic Development for Latin America,* (St. Martin's Press, 1961).

8.   Several protectionist arguments are clearly stated by B. N. Ganguli, "Principles of Protection in the Context of Underdeveloped Countries," *Indian Economic Review,* February, 1952; Gunnar Myrdal, *An International Economy,* (Harper & Brothers, 1956), chap. XIII; Raúl Prebisch, "Commercial Policy in the Underdeveloped Countries," *American Economic Review, Papers and Proceedings,* May, 1959. A balanced appraisal of some relevant arguments is presented by John Black, "Arguments for Tariffs," *Oxford Economic Papers,* June, 1959. H. W. Arndt's "External Economies in Economic Growth," *Economic Record,* November, 1955, provides a useful background to the external economies argument. Modern variants of the "Manoilesco-type" of argument for protection [Mihail Manoilesco, *The Theory of Protection and International Trade,* (P. S. King, 1931)] are formulated by W. A. Lewis, "Economic Development with Un-

limited Supplies of Labour," *Manchester School of Economic and Social Studies*, May, 1954, and E. E. Hagen, "An Economic Justification for Protection," *Quarterly Journal of Economics*, November, 1958.

From the many writings on the "balanced growth" doctrine, the implications for the protectionist argument may be most readily recognized in the following: Ragnar Nurkse, "The Conflict between 'Balanced Growth' and International Specialization," in *Lectures on Economic Development* (Istanbul, 1958) [reprinted in *Equilibrium and Growth in the World Economy*, (Harvard University Press, 1961)]; M. Fleming, "External Economies and the Doctrine of Balanced Growth," *Economic Journal*, June, 1955; John Sheahan, "International Specialization and the Concept of Balanced Growth," *Quarterly Journal of Economics*, May, 1958; Tibor Scitovsky, "Growth—Balanced or Unbalanced?" *The Allocation of Economic Resources, Essays in Honor of B. F. Haley* (Stanford University Press, 1959); Paul Streeten, "Unbalanced Growth," *Oxford Economic Papers*, June, 1959, (expanded version appears as chap. 5 in Streeten's *Economic Integration*); J. M. Montias, "Balanced Growth and International Specialization: A Diagrammatic Analysis," *Oxford Economic Papers*, June, 1961.

Among the increasing number of studies of customs unions or other preferential trading arrangements, several deserve mention for their analytical content: Jacob Viner, *The Customs Union Issue*, (Carnegie Endowment for International Peace, 1950); J. E. Meade, *The Theory of Customs Unions*, (North-Holland Publishing Co., 1955); R. G. Lipsey, "The Theory of Customs Unions: A General Survey," *Economic Journal*, September, 1960; H. G. Johnson, "The Economic Theory of Customs Union," *Pakistan Economic Journal*, March, 1960; R. L. Allen, "Integration in Less Developed Areas," *Kyklos*, vol. XIV, No. 3, 1961; Hal B. Lary, "Economic Development and the Capacity to Import—International Policies," in *Lectures on Economic Development*, (Istanbul, 1958); T. Scitovsky, "International Trade and

Economic Integration as a Means of Overcoming the Disadvantages of a Small Nation," E. A. G. Robinson, ed., *Economic Consequences of the Size of Nations,* (Macmillan & Co., 1960); Bela Balassa, *The Theory of Economic Integration,* (Richard D. Irwin, Inc., 1961), with selected bibliography; Paul Streeten, *Economic Integration,* (A. W. Sythoff, 1961).

9.   A diversity of opinion is to be found on the "Singer-Prebisch-Myrdal" argument that underdevelopment is due to forces of the international trading system. The most comprehensive statement of Raúl Prebisch's view appears in the Economic Commission for Latin America's *Economic Development of Latin America and Its Principal Problems,* (United Nations, 1950), and *Economic Survey of Latin America, 1949,* (United Nations, 1950). The unequal distribution of gains from trade argument is also presented by H. W. Singer, "The Distribution of Gains Between Investing and Borrowing Countries," *American Economic Review, Papers and Proceedings,* May, 1950. Gunnar Myrdal's criticism of the traditional view of "growth through trade" is presented in his *An International Economy* (Harper & Brothers, 1956), *Rich Lands and Poor* (Harper & Brothers, 1957), and in a condensed form in his *Development and Underdevelopment: A Note on the Mechanism of National and International Economic Inequality,* (National Bank of Egypt, 1956). In addition, some provocative arguments against the traditional view are to be found in T. Balogh, "Some Theoretical Problems of Post-War Foreign Investment," *Oxford Economic Papers,* March, 1945; Hla Myint, "An Interpretation of Economic Backwardness," *Oxford Economic Papers,* June, 1954; Folke Hilgerdt, "Uses and Limitations of International Trade in Overcoming Inequalities in World Distribution of Population and Resources," United Nations, *Proceedings of the World Population Conference* (1955); and in Paul A. Baran's "On the Political Economy of Backwardness," *Manchester School of Economic and Social Studies,* January, 1952, and *The Political Economy of Growth,* (Monthly

Review Press, 1957). A more temperate, but still rather pessimistic view, is presented by Ragnar Nurkse in his Istanbul lecture and the Wicksell Lectures (see section 4, above). On the other side, Gottfried Haberler's Cairo lectures and the two articles by A. K. Cairncross (see section 4, above) provide a substantial case for the contribution that trade can make to development.

The following articles also help to delineate the main issues: A. N. McLeod, "Trade and Investment in Underdeveloped Areas: A Comment," *American Economic Review,* June, 1951; Hla Myint, "The Gains from International Trade and the Backward Countries," *Review of Economic Studies,* vol. XXII (2), No. 58 (1954-55); D. C. North, "Location Theory and Regional Economic Growth," *Journal of Political Economy,* June, 1955; R. E. Baldwin, "Patterns of Development in Newly Settled Regions," *Manchester School of Economic and Social Studies,* May, 1956; Dudley Seers, "An Approach to the Short-Period Analysis of Primary-Producing Economies," *Oxford Economic Papers,* February, 1959; Boris C. Swerling, "Some Interrelationships between Agricultural Trade and Economic Development," *Kyklos,* vol. XIV, No. 3 (1961).

For some historical perspective on the developmental effects of export industries, it is useful to consult A. J. Youngson, *Possibilities of Economic Progress,* (Cambridge University Press, 1959); J. R. T. Hughes, "Foreign Trade and Balanced Growth: The Historical Framework," *American Economic Review, Papers and Proceedings,* May, 1959; J. V. Levin, *The Export Economies,* (Harvard University Press, 1960); K. E. Berrill, "International Trade and the Rate of Economic Growth," *Economic History Review,* April, 1960.

# Index

Absorption approach, 66-67, 78, 80-82

Absorptive capacity, 91-92, 139

Agriculture, 89, 139-141, 173

Alexander, S. S., 67 n., 81 n.

Allen, R. G. D., 41 n.

Allen, W. R., 46 n.

Alter, G. M., 109 n.

"Anti-trade-biased" growth, 22 n.

Arndt, H. W., 106 n., 132 n.

Autonomous changes, 20, 50

Balanced growth, 128, 131

Balance of payments, 64 ff.
  and capital accumulation, 64 ff., 88
  and national income, 66
  deficit, 65, 67, 70
  equilibruim in, 64-65, 70, 76

Balassa, B., 146 n.

Baldwin, R. E., 59 n., 178 n.

Balogh, T., 94 n., 96 n., 105 n.

Barter terms of trade, *see* Terms of trade

Bastable, C. F., 50 n., 52, 126

Bauer, P. T., 189 n.

Berrill, K. E., 160 n.

Bhagwati, J., 28 n., 49 n., 50 n.

Bias in consumption, 30 ff.

Bias in production, 22 ff.

Bias, over-all, 34-38
  and terms of trade, 46-49
  degree of, 35
  summary table of, 38
  types of, 35-38

"Big push," 152

Black, J., 22 n., 37 n.

Boeke, J. H., 167 n.

Buckley, K., 177 n.

Cairncross, A. K., 187 n.

Capacity to import, 42, 54, 63, 121

Capital accumulation, and balance of payments, 7
  and commercial policy, 120-124
  and development plan, 84, 87
  and production bias, 25
  *See also* Investment